About the author

Educated at St Pauls, a maths degree at Cambridge, and a British gliding champion, John Simpson found himself a teaching job at Clayesmore in Dorset. He was very happy there, but the war was just beginning, and he had no wish to join up. His pacifist attitude inevitably led to a Tribunal, and the possibility of imprisonment. The situation was resolved by joining the Friends Ambulance Unit where he first received some basic medical training. This led to a position in an East London hospital which gave him his first real experience of the effects of war and bombing. After further training in vehicle maintenance, he was sent to China, a country which had always fascinated him. Here, in the Western part of the country at Kutsing, he helped to keep the trucks moving on the old Burma Road with its 24 bends and many bandits. The personal letters he sent to Jean, his future wife, form the main body of this book, and provide a unique insight into life among the Chinese at that time. Years later he returned there as a distinguished scientific guest with Jean, and found a very different country.

Letters from China

Quaker Relief Work in Bandit Country
1944-46

John E. Simpson

Ross-Evans

British Library Cataloguing in Publication Data

Simpson, John E
Letters from China: Quaker Relief Work in Bandit Country 1944-46

1. Simpson, John E. - diaries
2. Simpson, John E. - correspondence
3. Society of Friends. Ambulance Unit - History
4. China - History - Civil War, 1945-49 - Personal narratives - British
I. Title
951′.042′092

ISBN   1 874498 05 9

Printed by
The Burlington Press
1 Station Road, Foxton,
Cambridge CB2 6SW

Published by
Ross-Evans
St. Mary's House, 47 High Street, Trumpington,
Cambridge CB2 2HZ

Cover picture: F.A.U. truck above the clouds in Yunnan Province

PREFACE

This book describes four years I spent as a young man, working with a Quaker organisation, the Friends Ambulance Unit, first in England and then later in China.

Chapters 1, 2 and 3 are largely taken from the diary I kept in 1943-44. Some of the comments are rather light-hearted, but it has the flavour of life at the time for a person of my background.

This is followed by a series of letters written from China in 1944-46 to my future wife Jean Campbell whom I had to leave behind, working as a land-girl in Devon. This material is much more serious, and hopefully provides the reader with mental pictures of a country and customs so very different from our own. It perhaps also shows how someone like myself, with a conventional Western education, can adapt to a quite different culture, and come to respect it.

I think of this book as a belated tribute to the members of the Friends Ambulance Unit, who gave me a job in wartime that I could believe in. Other members of the F.A.U. China Convoy have written books on their experiences in China. One of these authors found that the experience had "changed his mind" on pacifism, and another told how he had "left his heart in China". My sympathy is very much with the latter.

I wish to thank many people for the help they have given me in the production of this book. Especially to Georgina Vacy-Ashe for the careful work she did in producing a legible typed version from the various diaries and letters. I am much indebted to Graeme Young and to my daughters Janet and Ann for many helpful discussions during the progress of the text; to Margaret Downing for her work on the maps; and also to Louise Hall and Chris Mortimer for their work on the formatting of the text and pictures.

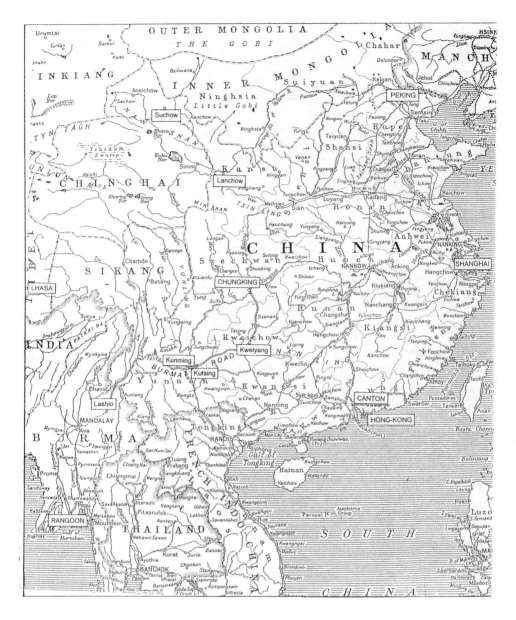

China in 1942

Contents

Chapter 1

War, Tribunal, and F.A.U. Training

The approach of war

After obtaining my degree at Cambridge, I devoted most of my time and interests to gliding. Towing my glider in its trailer behind my Alvis Silver Eagle, I visited most of the gliding sites in the country. In January 1939 I became an assistant master teaching Mathematics at Clayesmore School near Iwerne Minster in Dorset.

This boarding school of about 200 boys aged 13-19 had features which appealed to me as it was different from conventional public schools. Firstly, there was no Officers Training Corps, and the young headmaster seemed unusual. It was said that he had made two appointments in 1939: one a new school porter, who had previously been a lion-tamer, and (myself) a maths master who was another rare thing, a glider pilot.

My "PETREL" glider at Clayesmore

I enjoyed my time at Clayesmore. Most of the other staff members were young and enthusiastic, and I seemed to get on well with the boys. Jean was able to come and visit me, and at weekends I usually took my glider to a Gliding Club in the south of England, or sometimes tried it out on one of the local hills.

The room in which I lived was directly above the Biology Laboratory, always a scene of wild activity, under Humphrey Moore whose enthusiasm was infectious. I soon found I was spending most of my time with Humphrey and his biological boys either in the Lab or on field trips. In the evenings we visited friends in Iwerne where we listened to music or sometimes spent the time declaiming the poems of W.H.Auden in the the local pub, The Talbot.

In the summer of 1939, the country was on the brink of war. I was happy in my satisfying and rewarding work at Clayesmore School, and with my teaching colleagues. I was also enjoying a lot of gliding and used to say frivolously that it was better to fly without engines - aircraft only needed engines in order to carry the extra load of bombs! The deeper significance of this was soon to affect my life.

The Tribunal

Being rather uninterested in politics, I didn't take seriously enough the fact that holding a private pilot's licence would qualify me for enrolment in the services. Once the war had begun, several of my friends joined the RAF; and as the time of conscription approached, I had to decide what my attitude to war service would be.

I had been brought up "Church of England", and both my parents were practising Christians. I was a churchgoer until my teens. and still took seriously what I believed to be a Christian way of life.

Some conflicts with authority started in my first year at St Pauls School when it was discovered during compulsory test shots at the Rifle Range that I showed considerable promise at shooting, and was asked to join the Rifle Club. Realising the purpose of rifle shooting, the idea horrified me, and with difficulty I managed to avoid any further training. I also decided not to join the Officers Training Corps. Membership of the Corps was not compulsory, but those who refused to enrol were subjected to a kind of degrading physical training whenever the OTC was on parade.

As a student of mathematics, both at school and at Cambridge, I became familiar with the works of Bertrand Russell, and was very taken by his writings about the futility of wars. Although the Church seemed to have suspended the commandment "Thou shalt not kill", I felt I would be selling my soul if I allowed myself to be conscripted. So I decided that I must register as a Conscientious Objector (CO) to military service.

I was called to a tribunal, and in my attempt to justify the effects of my moral objections, I was led into explaining why I considered that war was an ineffective way of behaving. The judge was annoyed and rejected my application. The following letter to my mother at this time explains my attitude to the proceedings.

I went to the tribunal last Friday, with the result that I was removed from the register of COs. The attitude of these tribunals has obviously changed recently, as I had expected. I was hardly asked any questions, but was chiefly treated to a tirade on what a miserable specimen I was, and how absurd my views were. I had to pull the judge up on two points, and tell him that I disagreed with him, which did not have a very good effect. Unfortunately I got him into a position where he had to say several obviously untrue things to boost his case.

I was able to keep my temper, but he finished up with a violent speech of about five minutes, shouting at the top of his voice that I was a traitor to my country.

I intend to appeal, but it is rather a farce if the appellate tribunal is composed of the same sort of men. It seems almost hopeless trying to get people to reach a sane attitude to war if responsible people like my county court judge are so prejudiced. For instance he flatly denied that there was anything in the nature of an atmosphere of hatred about in the country at present.

It was at this time that I discovered that similar beliefs to mine were held by many members of the Religious Society of Friends, the Quakers. I began to study their remarkable history of resisting such accepted social practises as Slavery, and their record of steadfastedly challenging any form of violence and resisting involvement in war.

Fortunately it was possible to appeal against the tribunal's decision, and I was helped in my preparation for this by John Nickalls, a very thoughtful Quaker who was Librarian at Friends House. He explained how I had led the tribunal to think that my objections to war service were merely intellectually based, and suggested that I collect more supporting letters from people who knew

Comments on the Tribunals

AN appeal by Alan Pheasey against the decision of the London tribunal that he should be employed in agriculture or forestry has resulted in the Appellate Tribunal placing his name on the Military Service Register for non-combatant duties only.

   *   *   *

IN connexion with the sessions of the Midland tribunal on March 4 and 5, our observer at Birmingham writes: "In one case a member of a religious body, whose dogmatic objection to taking part in the wars of this world is usually recognized and allowed as a ground for exemption, was found to be engaged in munition work. Yet he was given exemption as a conscientious objector. In other cases this has been treated as evidence of lack of genuineness."

   *   *   *

TWO unusual cases, in which the applicants had refused to register under the National Service (Armed Forces) Act were heard by the Appellate Tribunal for England and Wales recently.

In one case, that of Mr. R. J. Porcas, Ministry of Labour officials had discussed the applicant's position with him, by correspondence and verbally, and had provisionally registered him as a CO. The local tribunal, however, removed his name from the COs' register on the ground that they had not had an opportunity of questioning him.

The Ministry itself appealed against this decision.

The Appellate Tribunal's decision in both cases has been deferred.

   *   *   *

WE now learn that Mr. K. Makin—who, as we reported recently, is the first CO to be arrested for refusal to comply with the National Service Act—was placed by the Newcastle-upon-Tyne tribunal on the Military Service Register without qualification, and not for non-combatant duties only.

It now appears that he was arrested on Tuesday, February 20, and not on Thursday, February 22, as we reported. He appeared before a special court at which neither press representatives nor members of the public were present. This was explained as being due to his arrest having taken place between court days.

(Mr. Makin's case was heard at the Newcastle tribunal last October—on the same day that the chairman, Judge Richardson, made the much-publicized remark: "I am as certain as I sit here today that if Christ appeared today He would approve this war.")

January 27, 1940

RATHER BE SHOT AS PACIFIST
—Says Composer's Cousin

A MAN who stated that he would "rather be shot as a pacifist" than be "killed in an attempt to kill," was exempted from military service by Bristol Conscientious Objectors' Tribunal yesterday.

The tribunal made it a condition that he should undertake ambulance or other humanitarian work.

He was Edward Miles Vaughan Williams, of Littlehampton, Sussex, a cousin of the composer.

He said that while at Wadham College he had been responsible for efforts to organise the Oxford ambulance unit.

"I have only one life to lose," his statement to the tribunal declared, "and I intend to be sure that it is lost in an attempt to achieve what I consider to be a good end.

"To be killed in an attempt to kill would not be in accordance with this principle. I would rather be shot as a pacifist against the wall dying ineffectively, perhaps, but at least honourably."

NO BOUNDARIES

Another objector said he could not recognise countries as having boundaries.

Judge Wethered: Therefore it makes no difference whether the Finns retain their independence or are absorbed in Russia?—That's right.

Or England being absorbed in Russia or overrun by Germany?—England I consider the same as any other country.

The applicant, Ernest Robert Tanner, said he considered every political system fundamentally the same. The fittest man got to the top.

Judge Wethered: Do you regard Herr Hitler as the fittest man?—He has been very clever at seizing opportunities.

Tanner was registered unconditionally.

Judge Rebukes Objector

When a young man told the Bristol Conscientious Objectors' Tribunal yesterday that he would not take part in any defence measures, Judge Weatherhead, the chairman, remarked:

"Some of you young fellows are doing your religion a tremendous amount of harm.

"Your interpretation of Christianity, pressed to this extent, makes Christianity impossible outside a monastery.

"The whole of civilised life is to a great extent based on force, because of a small minority.

"Now in Europe we have the same thing on a large scale because of the National Socialist regime in Germany.

"This interpretation reduces Christianity to an absurdity and a menace instead of a help to civilisation."

Press cuttings from the Tribunals

me. Also he thought that I might consider what other kind of service I could undertake.

I had a much more sympathetic reception from the appeal tribunal who registered me for land work or ambulance work under civilian control. Below is a second letter to my mother on the subject.

I attended the Appelate tribunal in London yesterday, and got a much more favourable reception. The result was a choice of three jobs to be taken up: (1) land work (2) ambulance work under civil control (3) full time air raid precautions (ARP). I am not to be allowed to continue in the only job for which I am trained and in which I have some experience.

As you may guess, the second choice appears the most attractive to me, and I have written off today to the Friends Ambulance Unit, sending in my application form.

The whole attitude of the tribunal was completely different from the Bristol one, which I can only think must have been due to my being wealthy enough to engage a solicitor, and much mention being made of St. Pauls School and Emmanuel College. Of course the case was exactly the same as before, but by the time the letters had been read, and Slazenger had given evidence about Gliding in the RAF, they had apparently made up their minds about my genuineness, and asked no questions related to Pacifism.

I shall be sorry to leave Clayesmore, particularly at present when I am needed there more than ever; but as I was seriously expecting to have to spend the rest of the war in a detention camp, I am fairly pleased with the decision. I should think there may well be plenty of excitement in the Friends Ambulance Unit.

Note that these letters were written only to my mother, and not to my stepfather whom I acquired when I was fifteen. He was a retired doctor, had been a much respected general practitioner, and was a churchwarden at the local church. Sadly my relationship with him was not a happy one. He viewed conscientious objectors as traitors, and having a CO in his household was very difficult for him to accept. I still have a letter from him demanding prior notice from me before visiting my home so that he could make sure none of his friends would be there.

I found out that the Society of Friends had set up the Friends Ambulance Unit in the first World War so its members could do medical work alongside, but independent of, the military. The F.A.U. had again been established in this war, and I applied to join the Unit. They told me that I could be accepted, but there was a long wait before I could start training.

Eventually the order came, and the 11th May 1943 was my last evening at Claysmore. There was an unnatural feeling about it, but I spent it in a crowded day of usual activities. After a morning's teaching, there was nothing much to do in the afternoon; but in the evening we had a 'Gut Club' meeting, with John Eveleigh, Hoskins, Payn, Reeves, the Hodgsons and a great many others who turned up for a few minutes and dashed out again. We fried eggs, and ate things out of tins, while Hoskins terrified us by throwing the empty tins at people from my upstairs window.

In the middle of the evening I was called out on to the playing field to fly the 'Buzzard' 5-foot span model glider. Zeylmans had his out as well: you should have seen the delight in H's face when they pulled too hard and the wings broke off on the tow! Ours got towed up about 150 feet, and landed beyond the piggeries over to the North.

F.A.U. Training Camp 1943

On the 13th May I arrived at the F.A.U. camp at Northfield just as they were finishing tea, and ate with Colin Bell who also arrived late. I started work almost at once, sweeping floors and was shown how to operate the boiler-fire. The next day I did the standard CO's job for the first time - washing down the latrines, and much cleaning of bunk houses. I ran round the lake for the first time before breakfast, feeling rather self-conscious about it, and returning very much out of breath.

When the Camp started properly with all 60 members on the Monday, I was interested to observe my reactions to all sorts of novel activities. One was drill. We had about half-an-hour of marching and drilling each morning, and I found it interesting to learn how to perform the different operations, but difficult to stand rigidly to attention without scratching or talking occasionally. Route-marching was seldom boring, as it was all through pleasant country, and a large variety of songs were produced. However, one did get tired of 'Sussex by the Sea'. This started with the hated bugle call at about 12.30 a.m. It was a slight relief to be told we were going on a route march instead of the usual mental strain of manoeuvres. But there were unpleasant moments, such as the few minutes spent at the double just before our rest at Barnsley Hall Hospital.

P.T. (physical training) was no novelty, but it was about ten years since I had last done it. Sometimes the games which followed were rather a trial, and I was often amazed at the seriousness and intenseness of some of the players. The weather was fine, and it was often pleasant to get a cold shower after a hot game. As time went on, the morning run became a habit, and on two or three occasions I enjoyed very much dashing in and out of the trees in the mist, with the sun just rising.

The day was always very full from 7 a.m. to 10.30 p.m. and I slept extraordinarily well, just like a child. Sometimes the piercing alarm note of the bugle went in the middle of the night and we had to get up to see to the finding and treating of 'casualties' in the woods and fields. For the first 3 or 4 minutes I always had a kind of dazed loathing for everyone and everything, such as I used to have at Clayesmore when woken up by the telephone for air raid warnings. I was usually in charge of some kind of operations, but found the necessary initiative and appearance of assurance very hard to assume in the middle of the night.

Every evening we used to meet in the barn after supper for about 15 minutes 'devotional'. This was in the Quaker style, with long periods of silence, and I often found an extraordinary mental atmosphere which was quite new to me. I also went to Friends Meetings on Sundays at Northfield, Cotteridge, or Bourneville, and was very impressed.

Lectures happened almost every day, chiefly First Aid and Home Nursing, given by Dr. Rutter and Sister Gibbs. Some of Dr. Rutter's anecdotes were amusing, but Sister Gibbs usually went on too long. The best lectures were those on medical subjects given by Ray Mills, and the worst were certainly those given by a Lieutenant of the Home Guard.

There was an interesting collection of people at the Camp. About half of the 60 members were young and had just left School or University, but there were many who had had interesting jobs. Fulke Agnew had been in the Army in the last war and had travelled all over Europe, particularly in the Balkans. David Thackeray was an astronomer, and had at one time been Editor of the *Observatory*. All classes were represented, from a Max-Miller-like man who had been a booking clerk on the Railway, to Hugh Russell, a son of the Duke of Bedford.

My own section was mostly very young. The leader Lewis, aged about 30, had been in an Insurance Office, a Scoutmaster, and in the ARP. I was next in age, and then came Ken, also a scoutmaster. He had been in forestry for some years, and before the war was training to be an architect.

Stanley was a butcher at High Wycombe, and must have been about 19. Definitely one of the lads about town, and popular with the local girls. Although usually oblivious of everything going on around him, he was a serious and efficient memoriser of First Aid and Home Nursing facts. Another Ken was very keen on doing unpleasant jobs and tried to keep myself and others up to the mark.

Ullin had left Oxford after only one term there, and I felt very sorry for him, as it was the obvious place for him to have spent all his life. He ought to have been a Don, continuing his Classical work, and discussing metaphysical matters without discouragement at all hours of the day and night. He was much more interested in trying to clarify and argue about experiences of say, religion, love, beauty and so on than in the actual experiencing of these things. Rob was also about 19, but of a very different type, being I suppose an earnest seeker after these experiences which Ullin so liked to order about theoretically. He had not left school very long ago, but had done a short term of work at a Forestry School.

Lastly there was Ralph, in some ways the most interesting member of the section. He was the only one of the section who was a member of the Society of Friends. He was a 'birthright Friend', and had been to the modern co-educational Friends School at Sibford. He had the confidence to challenge the Camp Authorities; but they got such a bad impression of him that they refused to admit him to membership of the Unit at the end of the Camp.

A few things stood out from the usual routine. One small item which seemed enormously important at the time was the visit of about a dozen girls from Birmingham called the 'Arden Singers'. After a fortnight of entirely masculine company, entertaining them at dinner and listening to them singing was a great delight.

Towards the end of the Camp I got in touch with J.V. Rushton of the Midland Gliding Club, and arranged to go to the Long Mynd for a day's gliding there. After a complicated journey I arrived at his son's School near Wolverhampton where their Speech-Day was in progress and where his son was having his last term. I met the headmaster, and managed to be mistaken for Rushton's son!

Later in the day we drove to Church Stretton, to meet the A.T.C. officers who were arriving by train. When they turned up I was glad to see F/O Lewis among them, and I drove them all up to the Mynd in the towing-car. It was six years since I was last there and was surprised at the large scale of it all, particularly the view down the Swiss-like valley on the way up, and the extent of the moor before we reached the Club-house. On the Sunday the conditions were not good, and I didn't fly the Kite, but had a very entertaining day instructing on the ground with the training glider.

I returned to the Camp at Northfield for another week which included two fairly big events. These were the 'Commando Course', and 'Manoeuvres on the Lickeys'. The Course was a fantastic obstacle race for parties of four with a victim on a stretcher. It started across a field and fence, down a cliff, and across a bog, where one of the judges got stuck above the knees and had to be extracted by four people. Then we proceeded along the top of a wall, across a stream, another fence, and another stream.

Then for the *pièce de resistance*. This consisted of a culvert about 5 feet high almost completely full of water, and about 20 feet long. This was terrifying to watch, but when one actually came to do it, it was not quite so bad except for the point where the stream bed suddenly got deeper. After this was a long walk through the wood and then down a waterfall about 4 feet high. This was not too difficult, but the second one, about 7 feet high, produced a few more problems. Finally we merely had to climb a kind of wall, and carry the victim gently back to the Barn.

The 'Manoeuvres on the Lickeys' were memorable for me as I was involved in the their organisation, having the job of 'tramming' the party there and back, and later as second-in-command of the manoeuvres. I had a good deal of fun trying to make a map of the county at headquarters from the confused and contradictory information brought in by breathless runners. Shortly before the end, when our H.Q. had been set up conveniently under fire from a 'machine gun', I found myself left in command; and in spite of bravely exposing myself to enemy fire, was not successful in getting shot.

On the last day we had a majestic five-course dinner all miraculously produced on three gas burners and two clean sets of plates. At the end there were speeches. I gave one and made a presentation to Dr. Rutter. Just before the end of the meal we were told what hospitals we were posted to for our three months medical training. My destination was Bethnal Green Hospital, together with Hugh Russell and Barry Webb. After frantic efforts trying to get my luggage at Birmingham Station, we finally got to London and managed a taxi together to the Hospital.

Chapter 2

F.A.U. Service in England

Bethnal Green Hospital

At this hospital in East London, I was glad to hear I had got a job in the X-ray department, and soon found it very interesting. Mr Miles and Mr Brown were very good company and obvious experts at their job, both in technical results and in considerate treatment of the patients. I was surprised to find the variety of work done, and I soon found myself doing a good proportion of the developing of the films.

The Dark Room appeared to be one of the Social Centres of the Hospital and we had the Massage Staff as regular visitors for cups of tea and many others also came in. Rosemary was a temporary member of the massage staff and we soon got to know each other quite well. She also knew the 'Bel & Dragon' at Cookham and we went to some Promenade Concerts together, including a particularly fine performance of Beethoven's 5th conducted by Sir Adrian Boult. She had also had trouble with her parents and told me all about it on the top of a No. 9 bus from Liverpool Street to Kensington. We used to eat at Kensington and after the concerts sat in the gardens and made rather unflattering remarks about the people who were passing by. It was seeing her every day that chiefly made the first five or six weeks at Bethnal Green so pleasant.

I also had very much more spare time than for some years, as I was generally off duty every day after 4.30 p.m. and got Wednesday and Saturday afternoons and the whole of Sundays free. Every weekend I got out somewhere into the country, very often to Cookham where I met some old friends from schooldays.

Sometime in July I went down to Clayesmore for two days. I arrived on the 4.50 bus, and was very amused to find a 'reception committee' of about fourteen boys waiting for me. On the next day I took several classes. One was Cunningham's Geography and the usual lesson on 'Moisture in the Atmosphere' came out automatically with the ex-members of the 3rd form all miraculously producing the right remarks at the right times. Next was *Remove Algebra*, including boys like Hoskins, Priestley, Bradbeer, Anderson, etc, which consisted of the production of a problem to fox Cunningham, my replacement, on the following day, and a few horrific remarks about life in Hospitals. After break, there were two periods with Upper VI Biology, consisting of a lecture on Blood Groups involving my own blood and that of Peck. A bit of a scene was produced when I found it almost impossible to prick myself with a needle as I was able to do with other people. Eventually I got a specimen after some crazy sterilising of Hillier's hypodermic.

All the afternoon, as JE was in a match, I wandered around gossiping and visiting various clubs. In the evening there was a meeting of the Music Society, where we got our usual amusement from the Secretary's remarks and heard Schubert's C Major Symphony. Later I visited numbers of dormitories, making subversive remarks and drawings on the walls, and finished the evening at the Verrinders, one of the staff.

John came to London some time in August, and we went to the last three nights of the Proms. The evening I enjoyed most was the Thursday when we heard a magnificent performance of the 'Eroica' conducted by Sir Adrian Boult. We stayed Saturday night at the Slazengers, where the smaller brothers were also staying, and we did some sailing on the Sunday.

Soon after this I got a fortnight's leave. I made a list of all the people I should like to see and rather foolishly tried to visit the lot. On the first day I visited the Hodgsons at Tring, surprising myself by apparently producing some talent at 'French Cricket'. In the evening I went to Logandene and had supper with Neil MacDonald who to my surprise was getting tired of making aeroplanes and wanted to go in for farming. He has been designing agricultural machinery and I should think would be very good at this. The next day I went by train to Biddenden to visit the Hoskins. The last part of the journey was on the Kent and East Sussex Railway which was still a delight. Brian and I had lunch in a kind of old curiosity shop and investigated the village in the afternoon. The departure of my train from Biddenden was curious, for after we had steamed out and I had waved goodbye, the train stopped and backed into the goods yard to drop a truck. It then started off again but stopped once more and did it again. This went on no less than eleven times, while Brian sat cross-legged on a pile of sleepers and ticked off the number of journeys.

The next journey was to the West, and started with the 8.30 a.m. to Bournemouth where I met Payn looking very elderly and resplendent in a grey pinstripe suit. Naturally we had lunch at the Lucullus, then a fashionable restaurant. He can be very amusing when he feels like it and when I was at Northfield wrote an extremely entertaining letter. I can imagine him making a success of his chosen career as 'Armaments King!'

Penelope, an old friend, was rumored to be down at the Kennels at Clayesmore, so I paid a call. When I got there, smoke was pouring out of the windows and a very typical scene was going on with shrieks of dismay as all the smoke from the stove was coming out of the wrong end into the room. Later we walked up to the Main Building, and when about halfway noticed Machiavelli (the Headmaster) walking briskly across the South Lawn. When he got opposite his room we were astonished to see him run up through the window and this phenomenon was only explained when we got close and saw that a camouflaged staircase of stone had been built up to the window-sill.

Finally it was on to Honiton to see Jean who was just the same as ever. We wandered around, had a picnic lunch, and actually managed at last to get up to the top of the 'Caterpillar Hill' to spend an afternoon there.

Back at Bethnal Green Hospital, I was given some work on a ward. This was a change, the nurses were pleasant, but hospital etiquette with the Sisters was a bit of a trial. The main trouble was that there was hardly ever anything to do, and any job I could grab meant pinching it from a nurse who was anxious to do it herself. The ritual of the doctors' round in the morning always amused me, with loud 'sh's' from Staff Nurse or Sister if any of the patients uttered a single word, and the curious procession of Doctor, Sister, Staff Nurses, Probationers and me.

Some of the patients themselves were quite entertaining, but some were fairly ill. There were one or two amusing ones who had nothing much wrong with them, but complained a lot and were always asking for things. A little Irishman called Fitzgerald and an enormous Russian called Sisoff were the best examples of these. However, Sisoff recovered very hurriedly one day soon after his next door neighbour in the bed on the other side had died in the night. There was Smidges who looked like George Formby, and Tilley who always looked very nearly dead and had a horrible habit of sleeping with his eyes half-open and eyeballs turned right up.

Most of my time was spent watching the clock or in the 'sluice', the wash-room. However, I had to appear to be doing something when Matron made her daily round, so I started a habit of appearing to rearrange the ward library whenever she came in sight. One day I would arrange the books in alphabetical order, and the next put them into classes according to subjects. This wasn't very difficult as the two main classes were 'Westerns' and 'Whodunits' and curiously a copy of 'The House at Pooh Corner'.

At the same time as the ward work, we spent about two evenings a week on the blood transfusion work. Chosen from my group to do an actual *venepuncture,* I did my first one with great apprehension, but with immediate success, on the distinguished arm of Lord Hugh Russell. It was a great moment when the needle slipped into the vein and the blood began to flow. After that I dealt with several members of the Great British Public, with only one failure. That was an arm with very prominent veins which turned out to be very poorly anchored and slid all over the place beneath the skin with my chasing them around with the point of the needle.

After the work on the ward, I was transferred to 'Casualty' which was a great improvement. Instead of having nothing to do, I always had about three jobs on at the same time; and when I felt less enterprising I could always retire behind my trolley in the corner and test urine. There were about thirty diabetics visiting every day, so this job could be made to last all the morning if necessary. But then all had to have their Insulin, and I got plenty of practice in giving hypodermic injections. The two extremes were Mrs Marshall - just like pushing a pin into a piece of cheese; and 'John Poole of London' (as he announced himself) with an arm reminiscent of a cheap dart board surface. With him, there was a sort of crunching noise as the needle went in, and having got it in, there was extreme difficulty in pulling it out again. Sometimes in the evenings things were not quite so busy and we sat around by the telephone dialling 'TIM' waiting for time to knock off work.

The afternoons were spent in Theatre, which was of course much the most interesting place in the Hospital. I found this absolutely fascinating, although most of the time there wasn't much for me to do and I was merely a spectator. The first operation I saw was for the insertion of a Smith-Peterson pin in the head of the femur, and I was relieved to find that I wasn't upset by it in the slightest degree.

I suppose a great deal of the pleasure of this work came through the novelty of attending scenes which are popularly supposed to be intensely dramatic. Of course the novelty soon wore off, but the interest remained. It was one of the places where you definitely saw something being done for the patient, and there is always satisfaction in watching a skilled craftsman at his job. I can say that I enjoyed nearly all my time in the Unit; but the most memorable occasion was the evening of our one bad bomb at the hospital.

We had had a lot of warnings for some days, with heavy gunfire, but not much in the way of local bombs. On this particular night I wasn't on duty and had gone to bed about the time the warning went. I had been asleep for some hours when I was woken up by rather more vibration than usual and heard a bomb approaching. I am sorry to say I was much more scared than usual, being sure it was coming straight at me, and feeling very unprotected lying in bed on the top floor. However, it exploded without anything happening to the ward. Just as I was going to sleep again, George came along and asked if I would like to help in cross-grouping blood for transfusion to casualties. It was then about midnight and numbers of casualties began to come in. Two were very bad, one died the next day, and we gave one a transfusion and rectal saline. Then I went to Theatre and saw a number of unusual cases. I was very struck by a girl of about 15 who had a hole about two inches in diameter right through her left forearm. She had walked in to the Hospital like this on her own! Dr. Holmes couldn't do much about her: he sewed up some of the muscles, swabbed with antibiotic powder, and put the whole arm in plaster. Another was an abdominal case, and he dug about for a long time, but couldn't trace any foreign body. I stayed on helping in the Theatre until 7.15 a.m., when the last case was finished, just in time for breakfast.

Heavy Driving Course at Leominster

At the end of October, 1943, I moved to the heavy driving course at Leominster. The day begins with the 'Death Ride' to the Milk Factory. At 7.00 a.m. we endeavoured to start the lorries - usually one could be started by strenuous pushing right down the High Street, and this was used to start the others. We rode on top of the churns five miles to Marlbrook. I found it best to lie on my back with my eyes closed, concentrating hard on something else quite different, such as Elliptic Functions or J.S. Bach. It was still dark, and sometimes we argued about the stars.

At Marlbrook I had to start my lorry with the aid of a 'dope-bottle' - this was often quite easy, but the penalty of easy starting is to wait and push everyone else. Sometimes we had a wagon with no lights, and then our time-sheet started with '7.15 - 8.45 - waiting for daylight.'

When the engine started, I dashed off into the dark looking for milk-churns. There were a surprising number of them around, often on stands, and usually in inaccessible corners of farmyards. These 3-ton Bedfords would go along quite improbably narrow lanes, and it must have been a terrifying sight for any little car foolish enough to come along the other way.

One thing, we did get suitable protective clothing, and I often surprised unsuspecting inhabitants of Leominster when they flashed their torches on us in the early morning. When we first got there we went around greeting each other with 'Capt. Scott, I presume!' Fine balaclava helmets of *grenfel* cloth and white gloves used in Finland were part of the outfit.

After driving for about an hour, dawn usually tended to break, and I became quite a connoisseur of sunrises. One day on 'Ullingswick' we came out above the mist, to see the glow above where the sun was going to appear. On 'Tarrington' there is a glorious track called the 'Burma Road'. You go on climbing for about a mile, and finish with a hairpin bend and reversing into a narrow farmyard.

At about midday I would get back to the Factory with about 60 fullish churns in place of the empties with which I started and unloaded them at the 'Deck'. This was a large expanse where there was always an incredible noise of churns being slid, rolled, or chucked. When unloading, the normal way of lubricating the surface was to spill some milk 'accidentally' so the churns slid easily.

After lunch I either spent the afternoon 'Servicing' my wagon, (i.e. tying on the various bits which had dropped off during the morning, or been stolen by others since the previous day) or else on a delivery run. There were always two 'Herefords' which meant unloading about 50 full churns in the High Street, continuously obstructed by prams. Less often there were journeys to Kidderminster or Birmingham. The latter is a 100-mile return trip, so I didn't get back until about 9 p.m., making a working day almost up to Clayesmore standards of length.

I developed a useful technique for getting heavy churns up from the ground. Anything up to 7 gallons was easy, but a 'tenner' needed more special treatment. The best way is not to know that it is a 'tenner', but if you know it is, and it knows that you know, then the only way is to catch it by surprise. They are like limpets holding on to their rocks if you don't get them off the first time, and the only effect of pulling is to make them grip harder on to their foundation.

Driving Instructor at Clent

In January 1944 I moved to Clent near Birmingham to be a driving instructor at a new course starting up. The journey there was complex, with all my worldly belongings - a 'mobile' Unit Member with enormous suitcase and gigantic rucksack! I had some fun with the latter when I was getting on the bus at Bromsgrove. It got jammed in the doorway and was nearly trodden underfoot by about hundred schoolchildren who were getting on at the same time. After spending hours waiting at Barnsley Hall for transport, the Ford van eventually staggered in with a blown gasket.

When we arrived, Duncan Jones and I spent about a fortnight on two Epic Jobs. These were The Shed and The Road. The Road was comparatively simple, no solid rock to blast away and hardly any rivers to bridge or mountains to tunnel through. The Shed was a very different matter. We were shown some timber in the garage and told that it had once been a shed, and that we could put it together. After working for about three days, we discovered that it had been a lean-to shed; and after about a week, we realised it 'leaned-to' the wrong way. We worked on strictly democratic principles and used to stand around and discuss our next move for as long as half-an-hour at a time. The stockman sometimes used to come and stand and look at the wreckage with us, and probably never actually saw us take any action.

Then the Course began, and I found it a good deal more exciting than teaching people to fly used to be. Beginners seemed to have a fearful tendency to accelerate at corners, and a tremendous reluctance to use the brake to slow down if necessary. However, nothing very terrible happened to me except such things as bounding along the grass verges and going across islands at road junctions. We had a fine old Commer Lorry, whose rigidity apparently depended on the strength of the windows in the cab. One day, when reversing up the bank on my favourite hair-pin bend, two of the windows suddenly shattered with a loud report.

Life at Clent was quite civilised, and I used to sit in an armchair in the evenings in front of a fire, drinking cocoa and listening to Bach. Also there was a regular ritual of the Section listening to ITMA every Thursday evening.

One day a policeman arrived, and we all wondered who he had come for. Of course there were roars of laughter when it turned out that he had come for me! I was wanted as a witness for the police in a case of dangerous driving. I was a bit anxious at first, but eventually worked out that it was about the woman who backed into our lorry near Staunton, and that she was being prosecuted, and not us!

I wasn't very keen on this long journey and eventually got the Police to send a patrol car to take me from Leominster to Weobley. At the Court we had a very entertaining time, and the defending solicitor turned out to be someone I had met before. He cross-examined me for a long time with intervals to explain things to the bench in words of one syllable. The unfortunate woman was eventually found guilty of driving without due care and attention and fined £1 and (my!) expenses.

There were a number of memorable Unit 'types' at Clent, including BS who used to roar with laughter when he went round corners too fast. After his eyeballs turned bright yellow, he was taken off to Hospital, and was said to be happy with a long nightshirt and two books - one on Shakespeare and one on Syphilis.

BL, known as the Unit's Problem Child, was a notorious character, when from the first he missed the bus, and arrived a day late, presenting an expensive hotel bill. My chief memory of him is of the day before a fancy dress dance, speaking on the telephone to the local hospital solemnly asking if they could arrange to lend him a shroud for the occasion.

Towards the end of the first course, the long-awaited invitation to join the China Section arrived to my great delight. I stayed on for the second course just long enough to run into a cow, and left for the Middlesex Hospital on 12th March 1944.

Chapter 3

Journey to China

The thought of working with the F.A.U. in China had a growing appeal to me. I had heard that the F.A.U. had begun to move medical supplies into China. These had been financed by America and Britain, but their transport was not a simple matter. Everything was landed at Rangoon and taken by rail to Lashio and then moved into China

The Burma Road, which was completed by the Chinese in 1938, started at Lashio and extended through very rough mountainous country about 700 miles to Kunming (see introductory map). As the war progressed, the F.A.U. continued to use the Burma Road which had become the only surface route in to China. In March of 1942, the Japanese took Rangoon and the Road was cut. After this the only route into "Free China" was by air.

The F.A.U. still found medical work to do, but the members were also building up experience in running a transport system. The main garage and works were eventually set up at Kutsing (pronounced "Chew-jing"). Diesel trucks were still essential in the 10,000 ft high mountain route to Luhsien, but at Kutsing the conversion of other trucks to charcoal-burning had begun in 1943.

This was the work of the China Convoy that I was hoping to join. My education, experience with heavy vehicles, and some Chinese language training, made this a possibility.

In March 1944, I had moved to London to spend a few weeks living in a ward at the Middlesex Hospital preparing for the China journey. Pleasantly central in London, it was a time for getting injections and trying to obtain appropriate equipment. There were some extremely noisy nights, and I found it more comfortable when fire-watching than lying in bed listening to the noise, trying to get to sleep.

With some leave in April, I filled the time very thoroughly. Starting at Luton, then cycling from Hemel Hempstead where my parents lived, I stayed the night with Hoskin's, and met Patricia for the first time. Brian and I cycled to Dunstable, and had a sad time at the launching point inspecting the remains of the winch and runway up the hillside.

At Whipsnade I visited Doc Slater, the editor of the Gliding Journal, full of ideas about treating insanity. There was a crazy book on gliding that I started correcting - so full of corrections, just as much as the original. We had tea at the temporary Gliding Club House and watched about 500 'aerial barges' (army gliders) towed overhead.

Next stop was Winchester to see Ruth and brother Hugh, then to Iwerne. I cycled all the way to Wimborne in the rain to see MR, and heard records of the Sibelius 2nd Symphony. There was a fine radiogram, plenty of volume, and it lasted me all the way back to Iwerne on cycle, still in the rain.

I seemed to spend most of the leave saying goodbye to people on railway stations. However, when I saw Jean at Honiton, there were three delightful days at the farm. I said goodbye about 6.30 a.m., sun just rising, morning mist on the road. She disappeared into the mist only a few yards away. I rushed on and just caught the 6.50 to London at the Station.

In April 1944, I was at Selby Wood, preparing for departure from a West Coast Port. This was supposed to be very secret, so no-one knew we were going. However, a parcel of sandwiches miraculously appeared in the cloakroom, and everyone disappeared at the right moment into the kitchen so they shouldn't see us go!

We staggered on to the Ship to the sounds of the third movement of Beethoven's 5th Symphony. At first there was much delight at being able to buy razor blades, sweets and so on, and also to have substantial meals. I was sick for the first two days, and then I settled down to a routine of walking before breakfast, Chinese language study until lunch, sleep all the afternoon, and nothing in evenings.

The best spectacle of the trip was the sight of the Pillars of Hercules at dawn. The sea was quite glassy, with banks of mist at various heights, and the sight of the convoy gliding along in single file curiously impressed me very much indeed. The Canal was interesting as it provided some life to look at, especially after the desert of the previous weeks. Large birds circling overhead, 2-8-0 locomotives, and camels - to mention a few of the assorted local life.

We anchored for the night off Suez, providing some wonderful smells, and then we were off into the Red Sea. This was quite horrible, and I can sympathise with the woman who went mad at this stage on a previous trip. Several nights I felt very near this myself, and existed for days in what seemed to be a horrible kind of dream. We landed at Aden, which provided two memorable items: an ice-cream and two Wrens in tropical dress. However, watching flying fish helped!

Eventually we staggered into Bombay, where Bill Jordan threw his black and white straw hat into the harbour. Very hot and sticky, we went on shore for a few hours after dinner, and walked through the hot smells to Victoria Station. It was very like any large London Terminus, but with thousands of people around apparently living and sleeping in the circulating area.

Next day we went to the Breach Candy swimming pool just outside Bombay. The water temperature was 90 degrees, and it felt hotter in the water than outside. But it was very pleasant lying on my back in the water watching the clouds and the soaring birds circling overhead.

We left Bombay in the 'Calcutta Mail' express via Allahabad after dinner in the evening. We had the privilege of a large 1st class saloon with shower, while the others were crammed into a 2nd class one half the size next door. The train clattered through the suburbs, passing electric trains rather like District ones, crowded with people in white round the open doors, and some sitting on the floor with their feet hanging over the edge. As I went to bed we were climbing up between some hills and through short tunnels, and there was nothing much to see except fireflies dancing up and down around the trees and bushes. All next day we travelled through dry brown country, some green trees, but not a sign of green grass. At Allahabad, in the afternoon, the temperature was 118 degrees, and it was curious to note the burning feeling up the nose as this hot air passed in. Later we had a dust-storm when standing in a station; and when it was dark we watched a high-class thunderstorm from our places in the restaurant car. The next day went on much the same, and we arrived at Howrah exactly on time at 4.00 p.m. in the afternoon.

At Calcutta, they were waiting for the rains, and the less said about the heat the better. We were in a continual wet state, and had to change our clothes several times a day. However, ice-creams were available, and many rupees were spent on these. A good place was the Golden Dragon on Chowringhee, and we spent our last evening consuming Hawaiian Sunsets, the most expensive items on the menu.

On 10th June we left by Air for the Middle Kingdom. The journey started at 4.15 a.m. when we waddled to the Great Eastern Hotel dressed in four sets of underclothing, battledress, breeches, boiler suit and khaki overcoat, sweating very visibly. I weighed 97 kilos, so must have had nearly 60 lbs of clothes on.

We went to the airport in a terrible bus, driven very fast, with several front-wheel skids and cuttings-in. It was a relief to get out and find some coffee ready for us on a trolley under the wing of the DC3 which was to take us over the 'Hump' to China.

After a reassuring test rev-up of the motors, we left India and flew in a clear sky at about 4,000 feet. After an hour small cumulus clouds formed below, gradually boiling up to five or six thousand feet, so we had to fly round the tops. We found what appeared to be another cloud base about this height, and went through one or two cumulo-nimbus tops, where it was rough for a few seconds. After four hours, the big stuff cleared away, and we found ourselves over a fracto-cumulus sky, with an enormous river below. We came down below the cloud and flew at about 800 feet until we landed, where we had a quick spam and coffee lunch in a new-looking wooden hut. As we left the building, the pilot bent down and picked up a quite incredible insect, with red and blue wing-cases, which he put in a paper bag.

Next we climbed to 10,000 ft or so, with the most stormy-looking sky I have ever seen ahead of us. There were great cumulo-nimbus towers all around, and veils of pileus, some of which we actually flew through. I had the feeling I have had once or twice before in a sailplane, of being almost completely overcome by the scene, and realising that I should never be able to recall it fully or even verge on conveying the feeling of it to anyone else.

We went on climbing and climbing, and the 2nd pilot came through and started off the oxygen apparatus for us. We shared this among the five of us, and by passing it round managed to keep all the party conscious. It was quite a pleasant feeling going off, but I was anxious to stay conscious, as by now we were spending longer periods in cloud, but kept coming out into fantastic scenes. On the one occasion I did go off, someone else put the mask over my face. When I came round, I felt exceedingly amused and burst out laughing, which I couldn't help doing for about half a minute, much to the surprise of the others who obstinately refused to see the joke.

After the Hump, things quietened down and we flew for the next 150 miles at about 15,000 ft above a fairly level sheet of stratus cloud. Then we came down into it, and for 45 minutes were kept circling in cloud around the airfield. The next day I had lunch with the airport controller who said he had machines stacked every 1,000 feet up to 16,000 waiting to land; and as we were a passenger ship, he had let us down out of turn. When at last we came through the cloud, there was the ground only about eight hundred feet below the cloud-base.

The first sight of China was very good after India, as it looked clean and bright and damp, with real green fields. And I could see people in enormous hats and blue clothes working in the fields. The first I saw as the clouds shot back was working some kind of pump for getting water up into the fields.

This was Kunming, and we were met by F.A.U. members and spent very little time in formalities. All I can remember was being presented with a form entirely in Chinese which the previous people had filled in with Chinese characters. After some amusement and talk, I filled in my name and age in what seemed to be the right places.

We stayed at the house of the Postmaster, who was appropriately enough named Stamp Smith. The streets of the town were very crowded with rickshaws, pony carts, a few trucks, and of course thousands and thousands of people. I had a very good lunch with Wes Chen an ex-member of the Unit. One dish consisted of small eels, two or three inches long, looking like little snakes. This meal cost $1,600 (National Chinese dollars) for four of us. We walked around the town, and all the children mistook us for American soldiers and invariably shouted 'ding-hao' (very good) with a thumbs-up sign.

We had expected to go to Kutsing by train, but a Unit truck was leaving, so we all travelled in the back of that, together with three Chinese nurses. A Good Time was had by All, trying to speak each other's languages, and singing the Volga Boat Song in Chinese.

On the 13th June 1944, I got to Kutsing, visited the garage, and was glad to see all the trucks labelled with the Bass's Brewery trademark. It was 7,000 feet up, and wasn't too hot, much like midsummer in England, but the skies were decidedly Aprilish, and it had been raining. The rainy season lasts until September, then it is fine until May.

Kutsing is an important city, said to have about 20,000 inhabitants, and we could get a good view from a small hill nearby. You can see the city walls which form a square with a watch tower at the centre of each. The plain to the East goes as far as a high mountain wall, called by F.A.U. members "The Delectable Mountains". Far to the West there are ranges of high snow-mountains, extending I think as far as Tibet.

I now have my Chinese name: this is Hsin Pu Sun, and means something to do with vegetable gardens!

There are numbers of Small Tortoiseshell butterflies on the flowers in the hostel garden, and a few Swallowtails. I saw a spider on an orb-web, much like an Araneus, but nearly twice the size.

The railway runs behind the garage. It is metre gauge, the trains are very crowded and the passengers ride on the roof and on the sides of the engine.

The next day we were taken round the city, which is quite unwesternised. Our hostel is outside the city wall, so we went in through a Gate along the very narrow streets. They are just wide enough for one truck, and I don't know what happens if two want to pass. However the South-West Highway doesn't actually come right into the city, but is served by a busy road outside the North Gate. Most of the shops on this street are *fan diens* - places where meats can be bought.

The Chief Cook (photo by Jack Skeel)

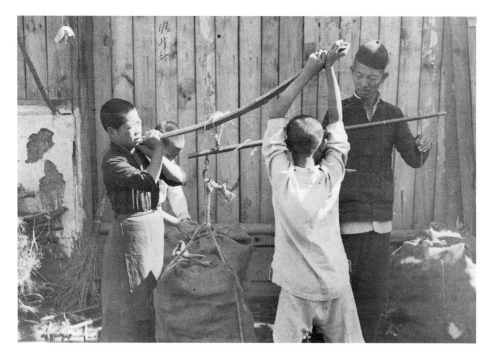

Weighing goods (photo by Jack Skeel)

Kutsing city wall and tower (photo by Jack Skeel)

Luxury transport - old style (photo by Jack Skeel)

Life outside the walls (photo by Jack Skeel)

We visited the military base-hospital. It was much as I had heard it would be, with emaciated patients lying on straw on the floor, and no sanitation evident. But it was being improved, and one of the wards had beds in it. It was in a Temple, which would probably be one of the few suitable large buildings in the town. We continued our visit to the 15th century, by coming out through the morgue. The coffins were just four boards loosely tied together, with a bamboo pole above for transport. Most of them contained two bodies, several of which had had the faces and other parts almost completely eaten by rats.

We also visited another hospital where the F.A.U. work and I was very impressed by the ingenuity which must have been used to improvise all that had been done.

In July I was invited to a Feast. This was quite exceptionally memorable. First of all we arrived at about 5.30 p.m. in the evening and sat around for about an hour cracking melon seeds and talking about this and that. At one time I was handed a piece of paper and brush to sign my name, but at that stage of the evening I wasn't able to write or speak Chinese. Eventually people began to sit down at tables and after a lot of ceremony and politeness about taking seats, I was horrified to find myself in the place of honour.

We were a very distinguished gathering, and there were no fewer than three Generals at my table. One was quite young looking, but the other two looked incredibly tough and business-like. The meal started with a lot of what seemed to me charming ritual, with our little china cups filled with the local wine. This is more like vodka than anything else I know (the F.A.U. used it for brake fluid, and I believe you can run a truck on it, but it burns out the valves very quickly). We of course took our food with chopsticks from central dishes, and started with a cold dish including some Yunnan Ham. New dishes appeared every quarter of an hour or so. Each one seemed about perfect in its own way. One other among the nine at my table could speak English quite well, and we all had some fun trying to describe what the dishes were. One we decided was 'Fried Fishes Stomachs'. We would all dip in at the same time on the invitation of the host, just having a little from each dish. All the time the wine was going down. It was difficult to decide exactly how it tasted as nearly every time there was a "gan bey" which is Chinese for "bottoms up". Every now and then someone would stroll over from another table and we would all drink together, or you would just toast someone at your own table.

Conversation soon got very flowing and I seemed to manage on a mixture of English and Chinese, with a word of two of French thrown in to fill gaps. I hadn't got any visiting cards ready, so had to write out my name several times in Chinese. Probably I invited all the Generals to come to Dunstable for a ride in the two-seater. One's wine cup was always filled the moment after it had been emptied and soon everyone was gloriously happy. Eventually there was the sad sign of the close of the meal with the sixteenth dish - the arrival of soup and a bowl of rice. Then some music exploded into being behind me. This was a one-string fiddle, a kind of castanets, and of course a Gong. We then found we had to sing a song! This seemed quite natural at the time, and I believe Rupe, Bill and I sang 'Poor Old Joe'. At last after about six hours the party began to break up, and we proceeded across the city with some Chinese friends.

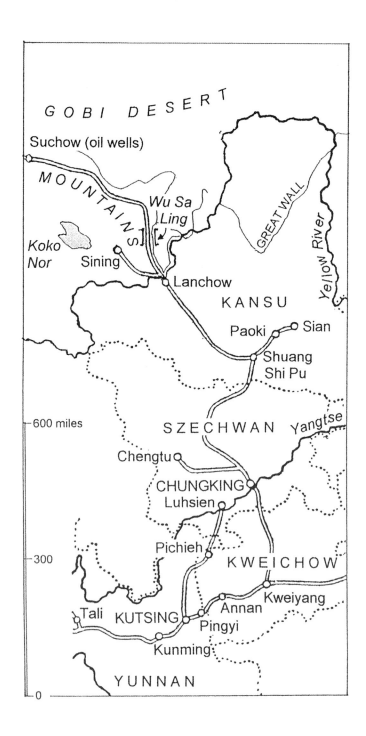

My working area in Western China

Chapter 4

Letters to Jean - first impressions

The letters begin on the boat journey to Bombay. There is one from India, and the remainder are from what was then called 'Free China' - that is the part of China not under Japanese occupation. It was ruled by warlords nominally under the control of Chiang Kai-shek's Kuomintang, later to be replaced by the Communists under Mao Tse-tung.

My base was at Kutsing, an old walled city about a hundred miles from Kunming. The air base at Kunming, basically controlled by the Americans, was the entrance to Free China at that time. At Kutsing, I worked at a garage on the Burma Road just outside the city. A FAU hostel not far away provided meals and a bed, although later on I tended to sleep at the garage.

Letter No. 1: pre-war comforts at sea

> Somewhere-or-Other?
> On a P. & O. liner
> May 1944

Dear Jean,

I have been on quite a pleasant ship for about three weeks now, and I believe there is a chance of posting letters at a port we may call at in the next few days.

It was rough for the first two or three days, but since then the weather has been incredibly good. As an expert on (a) Eating, (b) Sleeping and (c) Lying around doing nothing, I find the life suits me fairly well.

I spend the mornings doing Chinese, the afternoons more or less asleep and the evenings in various ways. Last night one of the passengers gave a piano recital. This was a very good thing, and included a Beethoven Sonata, and Bach's 'Jesu, joy of man's desiring'. I should like to play the treble part of the Bach on my recorder, but so far haven't had the nerve to unpack it. It is obviously impossible to get far enough away from other passengers for no-one to hear me practising.

With 4-course meals every few hours, and many pre-war luxuries available it is hard to realise what is going on outside. There are several others going to Chungking, but so far the 'Isn't it a Small World' department hasn't got as far as finding any mutual friends or acquaintances.

Since I wrote the above a few days ago, I have spent most of the time leaning over the side, wondering if the sea really can be as blue as that, and most of the evenings leaning over watching the phosphorescence at the side of the ship. One of the day's events is watching the disc of the sun slide down into (or behind?) the sea at sunset. Today we changed into Tropical Kit, and I got out my 'Wondersuit' with numerous brass buttons, belt and enormous flap pockets. Unfortunately they are slightly creased and of course we slouch about with our hands in our pockets, so there is now a rumour going about the ship that we are American Generals in disguise!

The Chinese study is getting on well, and some of us are now almost past the 'Have you the pen of my gardener's Aunt' stage and occasionally even can say Chinese phrases which fit into ordinary conversation. I am also learning to write everything I learn to say in Chinese characters, but don't know how long I shall keep that up.

We had another concert last night, with one or two songs as well as the piano. Do you remember the film we saw at Honiton last month in which Leslie Henson played the notorious Rachmaninoff Prelude? As an encore, the pianist played this last night, and I was disappointed when he didn't produce a notebook and count along the keys at the right moment.

I don't expect this letter will reach you for some time, but the Unit will probably let you know the whereabouts of my party quite a bit earlier. Don't work too hard!

Yours

John

Letter No. 2 (Airgraph): *from Bombay to Calcutta*

No. 1, Upper Wood Street,
Calcutta,
India
2nd June 1944

Dear Jean,

Thanks for your Airgraph which I was very glad to find waiting for me when I arrived in Calcutta yesterday. I stayed two days in Bombay, spent my spare time in a swimming pool, and had a very comfortable three days in the train.

I am spending a week here, and shan't be sorry to go somewhere cooler. However, there are compensations. I wished you could have been with me yesterday evening, when I had a chocolate ice cream soda, a Rainbow Special, an Ice, and an iced lemon drink.

If you had a map, you might see our train journey. We went via Allahabad, so have been right across the country. It was hot in the middle, 118° in the shade at one station.

Was sorry to hear it wasn't warm enough to bathe at Sidmouth. At Bombay the water was really too hot to stay in for more than a few minutes.

Hoping to hear again what you have been doing,

Yours

John

Letter no.3: eternal spring in Yunnan

Kunming,
Yunnan,
Free China.
11th June 1944

Dear Jean,

We arrived at last yesterday. After a wonderful flight above and through the clouds for about eight hours we came down through the clouds. Suddenly the earth appeared at only 900 feet, and it was delightful to see some green fields at last after the previous fortnight. The houses all looked much cleaner and brighter, and we could see people in enormous hats working in the fields.

This was Kunming, and when we landed, there was a slight drizzle, and it was pleasantly cool after the appalling heat of the day before. We are staying here two days and going on in a Unit truck to Kutsing. Had a short trip out this afternoon for about 12 Kilometres. Kunming is 6000 feet up with some interesting scenery, with mountains around, and enormous crowds on the roads, many people carrying things like this:-

There were pony carts with the wheels at extraordinary angles, and a few trucks packed with people.

Went for a short walk this morning. The people here are very different, as they all appear very cheerful. The children are delightful, they think we are American Soldiers, and invariably each one from age 2 to about 12 greets us with a thumbs up sign and says 'ding hao!', with an immense grin, to which we reply in the same way. The town is on a large plateau, and according to the inhabitants there are no seasons, but Spring all the year round. It certainly seems rather like that just now. I am staying in the house of the Postmaster, whose name appropriately enough is Stamp Smith, next door to the Post Office, a glorious building which appears to be open all night.

Can't get away from the B.B.C., as I am writing this at 6 p.m. in the evening. They have just played 'Lillibullero' and are now reading the 11 a.m. news.

Not much more to write about. I went out for a meal in a restaurant last night. This was very good - it is fortunate that I like Chinese food, as it is so completely different from European food. I can't tell you the names of things we had, except that bamboo shoots and sweet-sour pork appeared among other things. The meal cost 750 dollars, about four months pay!

I hope the buffaloes and whatever else you are using for ploughing in the Far West are not giving trouble.

Yours

John

Letter no.4: with a new Chinese name

> Kutsing,
> Yunnan,
> Free China
> 20/6/44

Dear Jean,

Thanks for your Airgraph of 20/5/44 which arrived at Kutsing on Friday. The letters you got from the F.A.U. were relayed cables I sent, perhaps some of mine have arrived by now. I'm glad the clock has arrived.

Have been at Kutsing over a week now, and shall be here for two months or so. Very pleasant place, over 7000 feet up, mountains in the distance. Climbed hill behind the town on Sunday, country looks like pieces of green glass fitted together - mostly terraced paddy fields about the size of tennis courts.

Our garage and hostel are just outside the North Gate of the town. Very Chinese-looking gate, and high wall around the town, which has streets just wide enough for one car, shops open out on the street all along with signs hanging down. I have now got my Chinese name which is Hsin Pu Sun, written as on the left of the card, and am learning a bit more of the language, also being an utter hog overeating on Chinese Food.

So things are going very well, hoping you will continue to write whenever you can.

yours

John

Garage at Kutsing

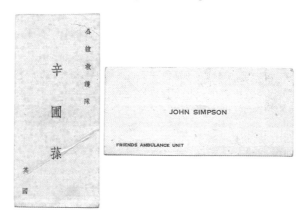

Visiting card - Chinese name Hsin Pu Sun (centre-left)

Letter No. 5 (Airgraph): The Feast - as guest of honour

Kutsing
Yunnan
5th July 1944

Dear Jean,

I am writing another airgraph in the hope that there may be more on the way from you. Incidentally you can send Air Letters (special form with 6d stamp) to the <u>India address</u>. Quite a lot of things have happened since I wrote a fortnight ago. One of the most remarkable happened last Sunday evening when I was invited to a Feast in the Town. This lasted about 6 hours and we had 16 courses. After politely taking a lower seat, I was horrified to find myself eventually in the place of honour next to the Host. There were 3 Chinese Generals at my table, so we were a distinguished gathering. There was a lot of strong local wine going around, and a Good Time was Had by All. Later one of the Generals and I sang a song, and many speeches were made. Yesterday we had a holiday to celebrate the 4th of July, but I went out about 80 Km. along the Road with someone else to buy charcoal. This was very entertaining, with hours of bargaining and shouting among crowds of people. At the second place we stopped there were about 20 children and 2 pigs which kept on getting caught in the weighing tackle!

yours

John

Letter No. 6: first days on the Burma Road

Kutsing,
Yunnan,
Free China
12th July 1944

Dear Jean,

I was very glad to get another airgraph from you yesterday (dated 17.6.44). I suppose by now the haymaking will be over, and I hope the clock has been able to take the strain of so many early risings! Did I tell you last week that you can send Air Letters, 6d. stamp, to the Calcutta address. This is better value than airgraphs, but I can't write back this way.

One day last week I had my first day on the Road, when I took a truck to the next town about 50 miles away. We had three mechanical troubles, but managed to put them right, and eventually got home at 11.00 p.m. Most of the way was among the mountains, climbed about 3000 feet at one place. A fine road high up along ridges, with lakes and paddy fields visible far below through the gaps in the clouds. Brilliant red soil, and mountains with cultivation terraces, almost up to the tops. It rained a bit, but we had a fine spell at the other end, and most of the way back.

yours

John

Letter No. 7: *a long way from flying bombs*

> Kutsing,
> Yunnan,
> 19th July 1944

Dear Jean,

We have got our home-grown electric light going again this evening, after about a week's moving around with candles. Nothing very special has happened this last week, and I spent a long weekend on my bed reading. A party went out to get to a Pagoda we can just see on what we call the Delectable Mountains, and returned fairly soon, as it turned out to be 12 miles each way. This morning I walked up to the Garage with a Chinese soldier, who could speak quite good English - it made me feel I ought to be able to speak a bit more Chinese. I have supper about 7.45 p.m. We had a very queer sunset at Kutsing, with quite an original set of colours and now I can hear the frogs croaking all around the building. They are particularly loud, and sound as if they are advancing from all sides.

We have just heard the news from London for the first time for over a week. I hope you aren't getting any flying bombs down your way.

yours

John

Letter No. 8: *beautiful China overcoming nostalgia*

Kutsing,
Yunnan.
Free China
1st Aug. 1944

My dear Jean,

You can't get much on an airgraph, so I am starting a letter for a change. However airgraphs are quick, and I have been getting yours in 4 weeks. Air mail is slower and doesn't reach the other end quite so often.

As a matter of fact I haven't got much to write about as I have been in bed for the past week with a kind of 'flu'. I got up yesterday and today walked all the way to the garage and back, 200 yards each way. I had a couple of days fever, which was a Bad Thing, but on the third day when I woke up I was able to appreciate the first thing I saw which was blue sky, a cumulus cloud, and a couple of Kites (birds not kites!) soaring up in circles beneath it, all framed in my window.

I spent most of the next day on my back looking at the dead bed-bugs above, which fall on my mosquito net from the upper bunk! After that I have been reading nearly all the F.A.U. Kutsing library.

I expected to miss a few people when I left England, but am also horrified to find I want to see some places again. A lot of these books were about parts of England, and a terrible number seemed to mention with approval places where you and I have been together, such as Holmbury Hill, Dunstable Downs, High Holborn, and the Downs above Swanage. In fact the latter was mentioned in one book by the author as the place he would take a stranger to England to introduce him to the country.

It was horrible, I got quite sentimental about it all. However, during my ten minutes out this afternoon, I decided that there was a lot to be said for China after all. At any rate this part, where there are no trams, no smoke, no newspapers, and not even any flying bombs, and the other refinements which go to make up our western civilization. In fact, I was glad to be back in China again, after a week in our Hostel, and to see the crowds on the road, and the boys selling bread and cakes, shouting 'beh tang, mien bao-aa', sounding just like 'Star, News, Standard!' There weren't quite as many trucks about as usual, but the usual crowds round the Checking Station. A little further along, down below the road, a man and a woman were making mud bricks. They are used for most of the buildings around here. They seem fairly simple to make, you just stir up a fine mud pie, push it into a mould of the right size, and leave it to dry.

The Delectable Mountains, over to my right, looked a bit closer than usual, with a fine collection of dark cloud shadows all over them. I got to the garage and saw some new trucks which had arrived, and started back. This is slightly downhill, and you can see the Town in front, with its high Wall, and the Drum Tower high up on the right. Further round on the right is the local hill, which is only about 600-800 feet high, but gives a good view of the town. In a sort of gully in the side is quite a large Temple, in this position it is probably well shielded from Malignant Influences.

Everything is wonderfully green, and the rice is getting quite a height in the paddy fields.

Last night I saw a sight which impressed me a lot. It was an enormous storm cloud, a 'thunderhead', of the peculiar, solid, top-heavy type one associates with pictures of smoke from volcanic eruptions. I suppose it must have been about two miles diameter. But the big thing about it was that it was several hours after sunset, and quite dark, but lit up about every 2 or 3 seconds by the usual lightning flashes. However, the thing that really got me was that about every 10 seconds there was a flash inside, lighting it up like a gigantic 'Chinese lantern'. It was really rather terrifying to see.

I hope you had a good birthday last week. One of our American members had his birthday on Saturday, so I was able to celebrate yours only two days late with some of his special iced cake.

yours

John

The way to the Delectable Mountains

The Delectable Mountains

Letter No. 9: *fauna and flora*

Kutsing,
Yunnan,
Free China
16th August 1944

My dear Jean,

We have been having wonderful weather for the last fortnight, fine mornings, little cumulus clouds later on, and it should be like this until next May!

Had a bit of a change on Sunday, when we carried a number of soldiers through the town to the Hospital. This is an old Temple and has wonderful grounds, very well set out with trees, flowers, little lakes and bridges, and enormous butterflies floating around. I still haven't had enough energy to walk to the 'Delectable Mountains', which look more and more attractive, but hope to make an attempt next weekend.

I am writing this in a chair on our little lawn in our Compound, in the brilliant sun; a Small Tortoiseshell butterfly has just settled on my paper, and just now I saw 15 large dragonflies all at the same time. Behind me I can hear many Chinese sounds, the boys selling bread and hot water and the buffalo carts with no oil on the axles making noises like the squeaking of railway engines going round sharp curves. Believe it or not, there are at this moment ten magpies (or something like them) perched on the roof of our Hostel.

yours

John

Letter No. 10: some real truck maintenance

Kutsing,
Yunnan.
Free China
August 29th 1944

My dear Jean,

Thanks for your Air Mail letter of 25/6 and Airgraph of 25/7 which both reached here about the same time. It was the first real letter I have received here, and I was very glad to get it. Please do write again whenever you feel like it, as you can have no idea how welcome your letters are at this end.

I was out on The Road last week with my beautiful new truck on a sort of rescue trip. I started out with a new back axle and a new engine for two Unit trucks 'pao-mao' (lit. 'at anchor') on the road. I found the first one about 90 km away in a bandit-infested spot up in the mountains, so left the axle and went on to find the second, which I reached just before nightfall. This was in a little village of about six buildings. The Chinese crew of the truck were glad to see the new engine. The driver is quite a character, looking like the European idea of a fierce bandit chief, and has been known on one occasion when his engine wouldn't go, to fall on his knees and beat the mudguards with his fists!

We had supper in a little hut with a pleasant Chinese family, pigs and chickens running about on the floor, served by a very distinguished-looking head of the house in skull-cap, long gown and slippers, with a little beard.

After a night on the truck, we started transferring the engines at dawn, and with the help of most of the village had got the new one installed and running by 10 a.m. Then we started up, and later met the other truck again. I gave him a tow to start him, and in the evening all three trucks rolled into a little town, where we all had a most tremendous meal as the sun set - eight dishes, all pretty good ones, I don't think I shall ever want to eat European food again!

I am getting some confidence now in speaking Chinese and carried on a conversation with some boys there for about 15 minutes. This was very funny, and we laughed a lot, but of course a large crowd collected as usual to gape at the Foreigner. It will be good to be able to speak properly, as here everyone talks and laughs with everyone else, with no European class distinctions and/or introductions.

Thanks for your enquiry about my proficiency with chopsticks. I can scoop up the stuff pretty fast, but am not yet a maestro in the art, and still not expert at lifting boiled eggs out of soup.

To finish the rescue trip on the morning of the third day we had my truck loaded up with 2000 jin of charcoal and while it was being loaded up had breakfast at a little table in the street. Translated literally this was: 'Hen Eggs in Bean Broth with Oil Lengths'. The eggs were more or less poached in this milk-like broth with lots of brown sugar. The other things were a sort of waffle, twisted brown crisp things about a foot long. Then we started on the last lap, with some bad weather in the mountains. The heaviest rainstorm I have ever seen was going on as we crept along the ridge which I now call 'Crib Goch'. (Please remind me that we are going there together one day After-The-War.) However, we all arrived in Kutsing again that day.

I hope you can read this. I am sorry the ink has come through rather a lot.

yours,

John

Letter No. 11 (Airgraph): butterfly country

Kunming
15th September 1944

My dear Jean,

I have been at Kunming about a week now after a fairly funny journey. Through some interesting country, but dark the last few hours, at one glorious moment both the headlights suddenly went out, and the horn jammed on. It is a change here from living in the country, but I shan't be sorry to move on in a day or two. This is very much a 'boom' city, and prices are high. Last night we had to pay the equivalent of £12.10 for dinner for two. All the things we can no longer get in England are on show in the shops here, but at quite fantastic prices.

My truck is still going all right. One day last week I went over the mountains 70 km to buy charcoal. On the way I stopped up on a ridge for half an hour. It was fine and sunny with enormous butterflies all around, a lake below of a duck-egg green colour with two little fishing boats on it, and in the distance a big storm among the peaks. Then down to the village, where, assisted by at least 40 of the inhabitants, I bought and supervised the weighing of about 30 baskets of the stuff, and eventually counted out 14,503 dollars. Last night I dreamed I was in England, spending a fortnight's leave with you, but woke up again in Kunming!

yours,

John

Letter No. 12 (Airgraph): bandit country

> Kutsing,
> Yunnan,
> Free China.
> 30th Sept. 1944

My dear Jean,

Many thanks for two Air Letters which I received this week. The one you sent with the wrong address will probably go via Tibet and reach me in 1945 or 6! I have made two more trips to Kunming since I wrote last, and have flown a Chinese glider. One journey was to take spare parts to a Unit truck broken down on the road. I slept one night on the way and reached him the second morning, when we had a wonderful breakfast of pears, sardines and bautzes - a kind of stuffed dumpling. After eight hours we got the job done, and in the evening four of us had a meal costing $1608. Had a race with the train on the way back, with the driver waving and whistling and the passengers on the roof shouting and waving their umbrellas. Had a disturbed night last night, with noises of machine gun fire and people being sick in the next room.

This morning I found a large hole in the ceiling, and 8 dead rats outside the door! I was attacked by eight bandits with guns on Thursday, but suffered no damage except three bullet holes in the cab of my truck. When they saw the fierce red beard of my companion, they ran away. I still think this is a fascinating country, but England still holds some attraction for me if (a) you are there and (b) there isn't a war on there in which I am expected to assist.

yours,

John

Letter No. 13 (Airgraph): above the clouds in my truck

Kweiyang.
Kweichow,
Free China.
11th October 1944

My dear Jean,

I am now in Kweiyang having a day off, which is quite a good idea. My truck and another did the journey in six days, which is quite good going, and I expect to return in two or three days from now. The first sight of the more interesting parts of the Road was pretty overwhelming, and the first journey really was an exciting experience. I can't do justice to it on an airgraph. We kept on going down into gorges and up over mountains in the most improbable way. The mountains near here are mostly very pointed, and I remember one incredible scene as I came up over a pass at dusk. I was well above the clouds, and in front as far as I could see were rows and rows of these volcano-like peaks, of a dark blue colour, with a pinkish sky background. Just like the scene from the 'Rites of Spring' section in Fantasia. We were on the Road every day from dawn to dusk and I slept very comfortably in the truck, with excellent food at *fan diens* in the villages or towns where we parked for the nights.

yours,

John

The 24 bends on the Burma Road near Annan

Letter No. 14 (Airgraph): a new photo, please

Kutsing,
Yunnan,
9th November 1944

My dear Jean,

I am back again in Kutsing, where the sun shines all the time and the temperature is just right. I expect the weather in England now is like that in Kweichow - wet, cold and foggy. This time I was leader of an impressive convoy of four trucks, and got through in five days as the condition of the Road is a bit better. Many people had worse luck than us and I have used a good deal of the supplies in my Red Cross Box. I find my hospital training enables me to deal with those who are still alive comparatively unemotionally. The weather was better, and we had some good cloud scenery. Last Sunday afternoon we climbed in cloud all the afternoon and at last it began to clear on top and we came out above into clear air just in time to see the sun set. Would you like to investigate sending a photograph of yourself by Airgraph. Ordinary photos are not allowed to be sent here, but someone had an airgraph one last week. Possibly there is nowhere nearer than Exeter where this service is possible (if there). I have got an old Polyfoto one, but would like another if possible.

Best Wishes for Christmas, in case my next letter is too late.

yours,

John

Letter No. 15 (Airgraph): crossing the Yangtse

Chungking,
Free China
11th December 1944

My Dear Jean,

Thanks for two Air Letters, which I received just before I got out of

Kweiyang. I believe the B.B.C. has mentioned Kweiyang recently, so you may have some idea of the situation there. This part of The Road was new to me. There are some good bits, one fine place where the road runs for a couple of miles in a little shelf cut in a virtual cliff, then it crosses the canyon by a suspension bridge and winds back along the other side. Further on there were some good sized mountains with snow on the top. We crossed the Yangtse in the truck on a ferry, and I am staying in our Hostel, on the North Bank. I don't know what I am going to do now, but expect to stay in Chungking for a week or two, possibly over Christmas. There is a place here where they hold gramophone concerts, so perhaps I shall hear some music again at last!

yrs,

John

Letter No. 16: real music - the Chinese way

4 Cheng Yang Kai,
Chungking,
Free China
26th December 1944

My dear Jean

I am writing a letter instead of an airgraph as I am told that they are now getting through almost as fast as airgraphs. However, it doesn't seem very likely to me.

Chungking must be about the best Unit section to spend Christmas at. We have got the big room all filled up with paper chains and irritating bits of green stuff all over the place. The food here is probably better than in any other section in Europe or anywhere - the usual result of having H.Q. here - it is certainly not the same for transport members on The Road or people with the medical teams. There were about 25 of us here yesterday, and we had 5 smallish pigs roasted whole for dinner. It was a good sight to see our Chairman served with a complete pig's head with a tangerine in its mouth.

We borrowed some records from the British Embassy and last night

Visa to Chiang Kai-shek's Chungking

The River Yangtse at Chungking looking towards the South Bank

were able to play Beethoven's 8th Symphony and Mozart C Major Piano Concerto, and then we listened to the King's speech on the radio, which came through quite well on a short-wave station.

I am feeling a good deal better now and was up nearly all day yesterday. Future is still uncertain, but I expect to fly to Kunming in the next week or two for some sunshine. The sun is supposed to shine there all day from October to May, but there are rumours of snow having fallen only 160 Km away. It will seem queer to do the journey in 2 or 3 hours instead of the fortnight it usually takes in my truck.

The weather here is much the same, mostly foggy, but with the sun just shining through in the middle of the day. Three days ago I went out for a short walk, and found a sort of roundabout called by some foreigners 'Piccadilly Circus'. Lots of luxury articles in the shop windows, saw a Leica camera, but didn't dare ask the price! I had a meal outside for the first time for ages. There was an alert on, and the restaurant I had meant to go to was closed. However, we found another one, and after the usual language misunderstandings got served with a fine meal. It was mostly rather indescribable, but did include numbers of small crabs and a duck prepared in a curious Chinese way. Somehow they get the bones out of it, and flatten it out, so that it looks as if it has been run over by a steamroller - like a brown shiny piece of cardboard.

Have come across another 'how small the world is' episode. I met a Unit member a few weeks ago who seemed familiar in a queer way. Yesterday someone told me he went to St. Pauls School and I suddenly remembered a boy of about 14 who was like him, and also of the same name. It will be interesting next time we meet to see if he remembers a J.E. Simpson who had a peculiar resemblance to me!

The China Philharmonic Orchestra is playing Beethoven's Pastoral Symphony on New Years Day at some hall in Chungking and I hope I shall be able to be there. I believe it is quite a good Orchestra although the last person I spoke to who had heard them had nothing more flattering to remark than the fact that all the players started and finished at the same time. Anyway the idea of seeing and hearing a real orchestra again is rather exciting. I miss hearing music a good deal, but here we are lucky in having a gramophone. The radio will get London well enough for news, but not well enough for music. The only permanent records we have here are of Beethoven's 3rd Piano Concerto. Do you know this well? It is much more Mozart-like than the complex 4th and 5th concertos.

Did I tell you that we are next to a Chinese Opera House here! This means that we can't help hearing some Chinese music. Although I enjoy the sound of a one-string fiddle being played on the street, I find this music a bit much. Every now and then a gong joins in and sounds as if an engine was 'pinking', and then the engine speeds up a bit and after some more misfiring, suddenly stops. There are a number of cinemas in the city, showing foreign films, mostly American. Last month they had 'Under your Hat', with Jack Hulbert and Cicely Courtneige, and this week we have 'Bambi'.

I hope you had a good Christmas, although I don't suppose it was possible for you to do much less work than usual.* I do appreciate your writing every week - don't apologise for what you say is a dull account of doings at the farm. I like to hear about it, and try to visualise just what you are doing all the time.

All Best Wishes for 1945.

yours

John

* On re-reading this, it seems to have a second rather rude meaning, which wasn't intended!

Letter No. 17: mountains and temples

Kutsing,
Yunnan
10th Jan. 1945

My Dear Jean,

I am now staying at a house by the Lake not far from Kunming, but expect to go back to work at Kutsing next week. It is a wonderful place, I should think it must be something like Scotland, except that it is an immensely larger scale, and the sun shines from an almost cloudless sky every day.

The Lake is 3 or 4 miles wide here, but it is about 50 miles long.

There are mountains all around. There is no green grass at this time of year, so they are all a reddish-brown colour.

Three days ago I went up the nearest mountain behind the house. This is between 3 and 4 thousand feet above here (i.e. about 9500 above sea level). There is a cliff nearly 2000 ft high up from the lake, and it is about 75 degrees slope above that, so it was quite an exciting business. I got round the cliff, but felt quite 'exposed' above it. From the top I could see one mountain I knew about 50 miles away, and a great snow-capped range over 100 miles to the North. I tried to come down another way, and got more and more frightened as the slope got steeper and steeper. Eventually I was reduced to sliding, holding on to bits of rock and tufts of grass.

Yesterday I visited some temples on this mountain. The approach to them is by a series of stone steps which are very high, at least 10 inches - and as there were 1,400 of them, I must have acquired much merit! These temples are very well looked after, with freshly painted images and flowering trees in some of the courtyards. The highest is in the rock-cliff and you get to these along a path cut out of the rock.

Temple and mountains

I was interested to hear you had been offered a post of W.L.A. gang leader! Why not accept this and work your way up until you get so important that you don't have to do any work at all?! No, I quite agree with your remark that you mustn't be a farm labourer all your life. I still sometimes have a pathetic hope that things will be more settled after the War, and we shall be able to plan our lives instead of the Government doing it for us. One thing I am determined about is that we are going to see much more of each other than we were able to during the War years!

yours,

John

Letter No. 18: life at the garage

Kutsing,
Yunnan
27th Jan. 1945

My Dear Jean,

Since I wrote last I have got back to work, and don't find it nearly as much of a strain as I expected.

There are about 20 of us here usually, 3 of us permanently working in the garage, several medical people, and a varying number of drivers. I like the other two in the garage, which is fortunate. So far I have worked all the time on the lathe, making various things.

I can't help remarking again on the weather here. Every morning as I shave I can see the colours in the haze above where the sun is going to rise. It is fine all day, and in the evening as I walk back to the hostel I can see the brilliant sunset above the mountain skyline. It never seems to be too hot or too cold. I'm afraid it can't be quite the same where you are.

I am told that Air Mail from China is now quicker than airgraphs, so I will write that way in future. Apparently Air Letters are still the best from England, generally under three weeks.

It is good news about The Road now being open through from India. Sooner or later we hope to get some new trucks through, and possibly even some petrol! Perhaps it will have some effect on the inflation.

Last Sunday I went up the local hill. Due to the change of season the country looked very different, not so much green, and other vegetables growing instead of rice. We have got a 'station wagon' here now, a Ford

Lathe work at the garage

V8 with a small wooden body. We are hatching a plan to take it out somewhere next weekend for an expedition to 'test' it out.

Last night we had an extra meal later on at the garage. We had some dehydrated cheese and a tin of corned beef, and I bought a 'dah bing' on the street. This is a biscuit-like thing, like a 12 in gramophone record, only thicker. The Chinese don't eat cheese, or milk either for that matter, but we now get a small quantity of milk daily, but for all I know it may come from water-buffaloes or goats!

yours,

John

P.S. I hope you like my new kind of envelope.

Letter No. 19: *serious problems and snow*

Kutsing,
Yunnan
11th Feb. 1945

My Dear Jean,

There's not so much to write about just now, as I am living a comparatively regular and uneventful existence.

However, you may remember the night I probably described last year when I was kept awake by people being sick and the noise of machine gun fire and in the morning found a hole in the ceiling and eight dead rats outside the door. We had a rather similar night last Tuesday. At about 2 a.m. our Water Tower collapsed and fell with terrific force on one of our buildings. A little later there were the two loudest claps of thunder I have ever heard, and in the morning we found the ground covered in snow. This is rare here and it was the first time one of our Chinese members had ever seen it.

All day Wednesday it was horribly cold and late in the afternoon we had a message that one of our trucks was stuck 30 miles away and couldn't start its engine. So I had to go out in our Ford V8 'Station wagon'. I reached them at dusk, and they made quite a scene. They were in the middle of the most desolate country imaginable, and in the road they had made a fire, where two Chinese children were also warming themselves. They had a fire under the engine to warm the oil, and another inside the bonnet, so it all made a very fine sight. They had been there over 24 hours, but had managed to get a little food that morning.

After 1 hour we got the engine going and reached Kutsing eventually about midnight, without bandit interference. The joke is that yesterday some Americans called in and told us that there was a big bandit hold-up on the Road 20 miles out on the following night! They can't understand why we drive our trucks without a man in front with a rifle, or a tommy gun which is so often in evidence nowadays.

This truck had on board a case of records from Kunming, and we have been playing them ever since. In fact I have found it difficult to write to you as I had intended this week-end, as whenever I settle down with pen and paper and the 'Complete Piano Works of Chopin' as a board to write on, someone puts on a record and I am faced with the alternative of insulting either yourself or Beethoven with the attempt to write and listen at the same time.

At the moment, I regret to say, Sibelius 5th Symphony is nearing the end of the 2nd movement. We have got Eine Kleine Nachtmusik, several Bach prelude and fugues, Beethoven Overture Egmont and Leonora No. 3, Brahms 2nd Piano Concerto, Tchaikowsky 5th Symphony, so we are having a very good time.

We have had nearly 3 inches of snow now, and this morning one of our members saw a wolf. There has been a sudden thaw this afternoon, and I am hoping the weather will go back to normal for our 3 days holiday for the Chinese New Year, which falls on my birthday.

yours

John

Letter No. 20: a new truck from bits and pieces

Kutsing,
Yunnan,
Free China.
24th Feb. 1945

My Dear Jean,

Your airgraph photograph arrived here yesterday, and I really was delighted to receive it. You needn't apologise for its being 'a horrid grinning thing', as the other two I have here (little Polyfotos) are quite serious and soulful looking! It was the only birthday present I received, and the best one I could have wished for.

I had an iced cake produced for my birthday (everyone here does), it had a picture of a glider on it, and the words '21 today?'. However, as I had to cut it into 28 pieces we didn't get very much each.

I expect you have got rid of the snow by now. I don't see how you can do much work on the land with a foot of snow over it. We have had some snow, and further north there has been a good deal. Three of our trucks

Original and new photo of Jean

got in this week after three weeks on the road, which is not my idea of fun. The fourth is still stuck about three days journey from here, and is expected in next week.

The truck I have been working on was finished on Tuesday, so I took it out to Pingyi on Wednesday. This is a new truck in a way, as it didn't exist before, but it is made up from bits of all sorts of old ones. I got to Pingyi, 75 Km, in 2 hrs, which is nearly a record for charcoal burners, and bought 5,000 jin of charcoal, which cost about $47,000. Lunch cost $1,200, but was very good! (about £15 at official exchange rate). The truck is not very beautiful, as it hasn't a front or top to the bonnet. The cab has dry rot in the roof, and sawdust keeps going in your eyes. The body is of the simplest kind imaginable.

My DIY truck

After the cold and snow the weather is back to normal, but on Sunday when I climbed the local hill, there was a good deal of snow visible on the mountains. This afternoon at the lathe in the workshop I was really too hot, and in the middle of the day, walking back to lunch, it is so bright in the sun that it is difficult to see. We had a very Chinese-sounding lunch today with water-buffalo kidneys, bamboo shoots and lotus roots, with of course rice and soup.

yours

John

Letter No. 21: The Festival of Excited Insects

> Kutsing,
> Yunnan,
> 4th March 1945

My Dear Jean,

Thanks for your Air Letter of 10th Feb. We have got some Air Letter Forms at Kutsing now, so I am sending one to you as an experiment to see whether it is any faster than ordinary Air Mail.

Your last letter made me think of several things which are missing here - the seaside - bookshops - and sweet rations (did I tell you we had 40 lbs of chocolate sent to us - the only sweets in a year - and owing to bad weather it was thrown out of the aeroplane together with the rest of the cargo to lighten it!)

Other things missing are that there are few concerts, and absolutely no Jean Campbells!

However, I'm not complaining about everything - good points are the absence of cinemas and newspapers and the incredible weather. It has now settled down much warmer, shorts are beginning to appear. I wore mine the first time today, and people are getting sunburnt again.

Tomorrow is the Festival of Excited Insects, when they are supposed to arise from hibernation. I saw several bees and butterflies today, including several enormous 'Swallowtails'. Also I have been bitten by a bed-bug, the first for several weeks!

I was interested to hear about the Chian Yee book. I haven't read this one, but we have plenty of little boys and water buffaloes around the place. I have read another of his which I liked very much, called, I think, the Chinese Eye.

Boys with water buffalo

Have heard some music recently, got about 3 bars of the last movement of the 5th Symphony from an 'ether-searcher' on the radio, and after tea today played some records including Brahms Violin Concerto and Rachmaninoff Piano Concerto No. 2. I thought of the evening about 100 years ago when we went to a Prom at the Queens Hall and couldn't remember the programme, but had an idea it included a Mozart piano concerto.

Goodbye for now. I hope you enjoy threshing the corn!

yours,

John

Chapter 5

Letters to Jean - almost a native

The spring and summer of 1945 involved momentous events elsewhere in the world, but news was very scarce in China. We knew more of the Kuomintang and the Communists, but it was unwise to write about this. Major responsibilities at the garage now fully occupied me. My spoken Chinese had by this time become generally intelligible, and helped greatly in my dealings with the workforce. The most important event during this period was the convoy north to Lanchow and into the Gobi Desert to Suchow to get petrol.

Letter No. 22: temporary promotion to Manager

Kutsing,
Yunnan,
Free China.
11th March 1945

My Dear Jean,

I have had one day out this week otherwise there would be little to write about except differentials and gaskets and connecting rods.

On Tuesday I took out a truck which we had just got ready to Yen Fang to buy timber. This is about 60 Km, but not so spectacular as the Road further on. It was very pleasant to get out again, it was the truck I drove during the evacuation of Kweiyang, and I took my old charcoal boy, Chu Ho. I am glad to say he can still speak hardly any English, so I had a day speaking Chinese for a change.

We started out about 9 a.m. and the mists soon lifted and it turned out a very fine day. Charcoal burners are very uncertain, and it happened to be running particularly well.

There is quite a lot of green stuff growing in the paddy fields close to the road, but further away from here the hills became more rocky and

The age of the charcoal burner

bare, mostly of a bluish-grey colour.

We got there in the good time of 2 hours and started arguing about the price of wood. Everything has gone up enormously, and in the end we didn't buy any there. We went on to the village and beyond to find a place to turn round. This was a track leading off between the marshes. We came back and found a little eating place, and sat down at a table with the truck just alongside. We had three Chinese dishes and some rather bad rice. The 'foreigner' had his usual amused ring of spectators to discuss how he ate his food, how much his clothes cost, how big his nose was, and so on. There were about seven boys and five men. The innkeeper spoke Chinese very clearly and slowly, and I was able to gain much 'face' by understanding everything he said and replying in Chinese. Very gratifying!

After lunch we found someone who would sell us some wood at a less exorbitant price, and three workers took about two hours to load it on. We got back in very good time, in time for supper.

Just now the Garage manager and assistant are away in Kunming and I am trying to cope with everything. We have about 40 employees and I only know the names of about 4. It is very difficult, as each has three names, like Jiang Liang Chin, Tsao Heng Tsay and so on! Fortunately they don't all look alike as some people think all Chinese do. They are quite a pleasant lot and some of them are very good at their jobs, and we have a good deal of fun with my few words of Chinese and sign language when trying to explain what I want them to do. Chu Ho is the only one who understands everything I say, apparently by telepathy. I saw him out this afternoon, looking very smart in foreign clothes - a white pullover and khaki drill trousers, and not wearing the filthy hat he usually has.

We have got an English member here who has done a good deal of Gliding in England. We have been talking about Gliding since 10 oc this morning (now 6.15 p.m.) and my throat is quite sore. He is just back from Suchow in the N.W. about 1000 miles away - or is it 2000?

I have just got your letter of 18th Feb, many thanks. I am sorry to hear you haven't heard from me for some time. I try to remember to number them so you can tell if any are missing.

yours,

John

Letter No. 23: the Manager experiments with welding

> Kutsing,
> Yunnan,
> Free China.
> 15th March 1945

My Dear Jean,

Thanks for your letter of 30th Jan., which arrived yesterday, a bit out of turn. It sounds as if you had a rather fierce winter. The cows' tails being frozen stiff sounds rather a tall story!

It is getting quite spring-like here, and there is peach-blossom around, just as you somehow expect it to be in China. However, a thunderstorm is going on at the moment, and in the next room with a loud crash the ceiling has just fallen on Arasawami S. Pillai and Jung Yen Ling.

This has been a much more interesting week than usual, as the garage manager has flown to India and the asst. is ill in bed, so I am having to run the place. I think I now know most of our 40 employees by sight, but still only know the names of about half a dozen of them. We have had five trucks in, and have sent four out.

My time has been mostly divided between alternate thinking out jobs for the various mechanics, tinsmiths, carpenters etc., and then finding more urgent jobs and trying to find mechanics, tinsmiths, carpenters, etc., to do them.

I have started to learn electric welding in my spare time, which is providing a good deal of entertainment. It is not very easy, and I haven't so far tried on it anything that matters, but content myself with sawing through pieces of 3 inch pipe and attempting to weld the bits together again. I hope to produce a surrealist chimney for the stove before the others get back again.

The thunderstorm is completely past now, and in all other directions there is the usual cloudless blue sky.

Several members are flying to India soon to drive new trucks in over the Ledo Road but I'm afraid I'm not likely to be able to leave here. It would be fine to see bookshops and ice-cream again.

I am trying another Air Letter, instead of Air Mail as usual. In a couple of months I hope to hear which of the two is quicker,

yours,

John

P.S. I hope it did rain on Saturday!

Letter No. 24: rain and green land

Kutsing,
Yunnan,
Free China.
25th March 1945

My Dear Jean,

I have certainly got something to write to you about this week-end, as two rather surprising things have happened.

1. I have been lent for an indefinite period a Grunan Baby sailplane. This is a good machine, very like the one I used to own, and I intend to fly it from the West Mountain of Kutsing.

Please excuse the mess which has just happened at the bottom r.h. corner of the page. It is not, as it might well have been, the result of shedding tears at the thought of not seeing you again for two years (when the W.L.A. transfer you to Yunnan!), but merely the stove chimney having fallen down and knocked a cup of tea over. This is due to the garage manager having taken his spare pair of socks with him to India, instead of using them to wedge the chimney as usual.

This is all going on upstairs above the garage offices. From the window I can see the 'ribbon development' on The Road outside Kutsing, and beyond it the walled city, with the Drum Tower sticking out above the houses. I'm sorry there isn't a window seat you could kneel in to write a letter to me, but if you were here, I suppose you wouldn't need to. It is quite hazy today, and the Delectable Mountains to the East are only just visible as a very faint outline.

I seem to have strayed from the subject a bit, which was Two Items of News.

2. I have suddenly been chosen to be Convoy Mechanic on the next Suchow Convoy. Suchow (pron. approx. 'Soo-Joe') is about 2000 miles away to the N.W. in Kansu Province. It should be rather an exciting journey, and we shall be away for about six months. Next week I am flying up to Chungking to see to the fitting of the engines, and I expect we shall get away in a few week's time. I don't know if you have a map of China, but we probably go to Chengtu and then up to Lanchow, the capital of Kansu. Suchow is another 700 Km. on from there, past the Great Wall, and a good deal of desert.

This afternoon I went for a walk up one of the river valleys into the mountains. We had thunderstorms on four afternoons last week, almost as if the Rains had come. It was fine today, and the river is fuller, and there are quite a lot of green things showing through in the dry burnt-up countryside. It will be good to see England again, where I believe there is green grass all the year round!

It must have been market day in Kutsing today, for on the way back we passed a stream of people from the town carrying all sorts of things, and a lot of them driving cows. They use cows for ploughing and drawing carts, but not for milk. However, around here more work seems to be done by enormous fat water buffaloes. I saw one today, tied by a string in his nose, walking round and round in a sticky mess of mud, which was being mixed up to make mud-bricks.

There are lots of butterflies about now, and I suppose we shall soon have to get our mosquito nets out again.

yours

John

Letter No. 25: sun and blossom

Kunming.

2nd April 1945

My Dear Jean,

Many thanks for letters of 25th Feb and 4th March, which arrived two days ago. I am now in Kunming, waiting for my air passage to Chung-king, which is supposed to come off on Thursday. It is very hot and sunny, I suppose it must be over 80°.

I had an interesting day on Friday, when I took out a truck to buy coke. This was about 80 Km each way, and the last 4 Km was along a little earth track up a narrow valley. This was just wide enough for the truck, with a drop down to the river on one side. The leaves were all well out on the trees, and there were quantities of peach and plum blossom. After the semi-desert country I passed on the way, it was a great change, much more how I imagined the 'Flowery Kingdom' ought to look.

Four of us brought a truck up here on Saturday. We wanted to get in early so we got up at 4.30 a.m., but even so, didn't get in here until about 3 in the afternoon.

I find it more difficult to write a letter here than in Kutsing, as I am sitting at a 1st floor window in Tai Ho Kai, one of the main streets, and if I look out for a moment there is a great deal to see. Just now a group of ponies laden with vegetables are going past, next an ox-cart, a Jeep, and a Buick saloon car. People are dressed in all kinds of clothes, some on bicycles, but many in rickshaws.

I hope you may be able to find my route to the N.W. on your map, places like Chengtu, Hanchung, Lanchow, Kanchow, Suchow.

yours

John

Letter No. 26: by air to Chungking

4 Cheng Yang Kai
Chungking.
7th April 1945

My Dear Jean,

I must apologise for using a Chinese envelope for this letter, but am making up for it by using a sheet of our best headed writing paper.

On Wednesday I flew here from Kunming, and had a very delightful ride. I had one of the single seats on the right near the back where the view is best. When we left Kunming it was clear and sunny, and as we flew along the Kutsing road I could recognise the places I knew. We saw the local train pass a few thousand feet below, almost out of sight beneath the crowds of passengers riding on the roofs. Later on the clouds got thicker, and we flew among great lumps of stuff with the ground out of sight. After two hours we went down into it, and eventually saw Chungking beneath us, with the landing strip on a sandbank in the middle of the Yangtse. At present I am still at our Hostel in the centre of the town, on the North Bank, but tomorrow shall move over to the Garage on the South Bank, where the Suchow trucks are. I have seen them, and they are nearly ready. It looks as if we might get off on the journey in under three weeks time.

I have spent most of the last two days visiting friends at the Gliding Club and taking more letters of introduction to more people. Next week-end I have an invitation to visit the soaring site about 30 miles to the North. Nobody there speaks English, and I shall probably go by boat up the Jia Ling River, so it ought to be quite an exciting week-end. I shall have to work hard this week learning various technical terms in Chinese. I have learnt 'thermal', this is, literally warm-power-up-rise-air-current.

Chungking is rather a confusing town to find your way about in, but I have now got a map, so with a lot of walking about, I find things are beginning to sort themselves out a bit.

Reading and Bristol aren't too bad to be in, but please don't go to Newcastle! Anyway, I shall expect you to be at Combe Raleigh when I return.

yours

John

Letter No. 27: Chiang Kai-shek in the vicinity

4, Cheng Yang Kai,
Chungking.
15th April 1945

My Dear Jean,

Thanks for your letter of 18th March, complete with distressing diagram of what happens when you use your strength on long-handled manure picks!

Things are still going ahead for the Big Journey, the cargo of medical supplies (12 tons) we are taking up has all been collected. I have got all our spares and equipment, but the trucks aren't running yet. One is giving trouble, and another has still to be dismantled and new piston rings fitted. I don't think we shall get away for at least two weeks.

We heard about President Roosevelt's death here two days ago, and yesterday every building in the town had an enormous Chinese flag hanging out at half-mast.

Last Sunday I saw Chiang Kai-shek go past in his car, but that's about the only bit of excitement of the week. We have crossed the Yangtse several times on the car-ferry, but so far nothing awful has actually happened.

Yesterday afternoon I drove out to Ching Mu Kwan, about 50 Km away, through incredibly fertile country. Barley and wheat is nearly ripe, and the very young rice is just beginning to come up in the seed beds.

It is rather hot and damp, and I was bitten by a mosquito last night. We shall have to get the nets out this week.

yours

John

Letter No. 28: a Chinese future?

Chungking
21st April 1945

My Dear Jean,

Thanks for your Air Letter of 22nd March. As you said my first Air Letter arrived very quickly and I am writing another one today. I have been numbering my letters so you will know when any are missing - I am sorry they haven't all been arriving. Yours seem to arrive pleasantly regularly, which is a very Good Thing.

I came over all sentimental on Tuesday when I realised that it was just a year since we said goodbye in the mist on the road to Honiton. It's been quite an exciting year, and has gone past very quickly. I expect the next two years will go just as fast. If it was peacetime, and if I had my sailplane here (and of course you!) there would be quite a lot to be said for staying on in this country.

I have been busy in the garage all this week and haven't been outside the compound at all except for an hour or two last night when two of us walked a couple of kilos down the road to the next village and sat for an hour or so in a tea-shop. A 'teashop' is not quite like the places at Honiton, but a little place open to the road with benches and little tables and peo-ple sitting round drinking tea and eating melon seeds. It more corre-sponds to an English country pub - in the towns they are usually full of businessmen. It has been very hot indeed, but yesterday we had a terrific thunderstorm and it was all right in the evening. In the evenings now there is a tremendous noise of bull-frogs, and we can see people poking about in the paddy-fields with great torches looking for something, perhaps eels?

It has been raining today, which isn't fair as the rainy season doesn't come for another 3 months.

One of our trucks is now ready, the second still has something wrong which I can't diagnose, and the third should be ready by the end of next week.

yours

John

Letter No. 29: The Great Convoy almost ready

Chungking.
28th April 1945

My Dear Jean,

We really are nearly ready to start for Suchow. Two of the trucks are loaded. It takes two to three days to load a truck, and they are now a wonderful sight. Each has 3½ tons of medical supplies, and then on top of that 22 empty 50-gallon petrol drums. They are absolutely festooned with rope, and now we are wondering what sort of time we shall have unloading them to get through low city gateways, and overhanging rock.

Of course one of the engines is still giving trouble, and we had its 'head' off this morning.

I am writing this at our hostel in the City - some of us came over on a Unit truck after lunch. It is very hot now, but is fairly clear today, and the Yangtse looked all right as we came over on the ferry.

Tomorrow I am visiting the Friends' Middle School, on the South Bank. It is up on one of the wooded hills with the pagoda. I think the theory is that I give a lecture on Gliding to about 500 of the boys, but perhaps this can be avoided. Actually it will be quite fun to be doing this once again. I don't expect to speak in Chinese as you may guess.

It is all very 'civilised' over here on the North Bank, and you can go into horribly Western looking restaurants and actually order coffee. (It costs about $250 a cup this week!)

We have got a good radio at the Garage, and on Thursday I actually heard the Tommy Handley programme. Yesterday we listened to news of the conference from the San Francisco station, and afterwards heard the first two movements of the Fifth Symphony. The news is exciting just now, and this is a wonderful place for rumours.

yours

John

Letter No. 30: on the way to Lanchow

Feng,
Shensi.
10th May 1945

My Dear Jean,

We have been on the journey to the N.W. for 8 days now, and tonight for the first time we are spending the night under cover in a building, so I am starting a letter.

We have done very well so far, with no real trouble. This place is 958 Km from Chungking, the old name is Feng, meaning Phoenix, but it is now called Shuang Shi Pu.

We have passed so much fantastic and beautiful scenery that I'm afraid I shall no longer be able to appreciate any mountain less than 10,000 feet, any gorge less than 2000 feet deep, or any vertical cliff from the edge of the road less than 1000 feet!

I'll tell you all about it one day I hope, how we ate a breakfast of poached eggs in sweet wine in a barber's shop at San Tai, and then drove 15 miles along a mountain ridge above the clouds, with a 20,000 feet peak in sight.

A fantastic mountain pass near Kwan Yuan, with bare limestone peaks like parts of the Dolomite Alps, then a river gorge with the road cut into the vertical rock side. And of course all the time there are crowds of people. They are a bit of a nuisance in towns. I counted 72 watching me solder a connection on a battery, but they are always cheerful and easy to talk to.

Chinese road engineering

We had lunch today in an inn up in the mountains next to a very fine temple, which we visited afterwards. We heard rumours that the war in Europe is over. I hope it is.

There are a lot of mule carts on the roads, and today we saw hundreds of camels.

Thanks for your letter describing your Easter week-end. I wish I could have been at church with you. Perhaps sooner than 2 years now! Will you perhaps also come to a Quaker meeting with me one day? If the war in Europe really is over, perhaps some demobilisation will be starting soon, and I may get back earlier.

Hope to write to you again from Lanchow in a week or two's time,

yours

John

Letter No. 31: a Catholic evening at Lanchow

Lanchow,
Kansu.
19th May 1945

My Dear Jean,

We arrived in Lanchow the day before yesterday, and I was very glad to find three letters from you waiting for me at the C.I.M. (China Inland Mission).

We did the journey from Chungking to Lanchow in 16 days, which is easily a record for Unit trucks. The last Convoy took 32 days.

After leaving Shuang Shi Pu we have had quite a bit of excitement. The truck with the petrol on it caught fire one evening. Apparently some bottles of sulphuric acid had broken in one of the cases and set fire to things. We had an exciting time throwing things off the truck and managed to save the truck and all the cargo except this one case, which was well alight. This case was labelled :

```
ꓷႶ ƎᗡIS SIHꓕ
ƎЯꓕᴎƎƆ Hꓕ⅃AƎH AI⅃OϾᴎOM
```

We spent a memorable evening at a town with some Catholic Fathers. There were five of them, all German, and they gave us a wonderful meal, with some excellent wine they had made themselves. We had a very extraordinary evening talking a mixture of German and Chinese.

Lanchow seems a fine city, and the Yellow River is quite a sight. We spent yesterday seeing to the unloading of our 12 tons of medical supplies. We also carried 66 empty 50-gallon petrol drums, and when it was all unloaded, it was an impressive sight, as the medical supplies were in 212 packing cases.

We are staying in quite a Western kind of hotel, where we get foreign food and even baths! This morning I had my first bath this year. This is not quite as sordid as it sounds, as I have had showers at Unit Hostels, and have washed in rivers and streams several times on this journey. It is all very pleasant, particularly after sleeping on the road, under the truck and in other strange places.

We shall probably be here for about a week, working on the trucks, and getting a cargo to take on to Suchow.

yours

John

Letter No. 32: picnic by the Yellow river

Hsi Beh Dah Hsia
Lanchow
Kansu
Free China.
26th May 1945

My Dear Jean,

This has been a very hot week, and we have just finished working on the trucks. We hope to be off to Chiuchuan (Suchow) in a day or two. We have delivered the medical supplies here, and have a wonderfully varied cargo to take on to Suchow. This includes some stuff for the Chinese Industrial Cooperatives, like machinery, and 80 pairs of shoes. We also have a large pot of honey and an altar. The latter is from the Catholic Mission here. I visited them this morning. They are also German, and we managed to speak in Chinese. They gave me some of their liqueur and also home-made beer. They have a very large church and hospital in the town and we are taking the altar to their Mission in Chiuchuan.

All the foreigners (missionaries, except the American Consul and one German) have been inviting us to meals with them, but this evening we are going out to some Chinese at the N.W. Epidemic Prevention Bureau. We are going to have a picnic in the moonlight, by the Yellow River. (This sounds good doesn't it?)

The people I liked best so far had a charming family of 2 boys and 2 girls. After living in a truck for so long, I was very envious of people like this with a home and children. We had a delightful afternoon and finished by climbing all over the truck and getting our clothes dirty! The oldest boy was aged about 6, and the smallest girl about 1.

Yellow River at Lanchow

Although it is very hot and dusty, I still rather like this place. At any rate it is always cool at night. There is a great variety of people in the streets and this morning I passed two camels with their fur coming off in great lumps.

The next part of the journey is mostly across the Desert (Gobi) and we may have to do our own cooking. This is also the Convoy Mechanic's job!

yours

John

Letter No. 33: the desert journey

4 Cheng Yang Kai,
Chungking.
Free China.
8th June 1945

Written at Suchow

My Dear Jean,

I suppose it's rather silly writing a letter to you now because I shan't be able to post it until we get back to Lanchow.

We have been here about 5 days, the petrol has been bought, and I have done a job on one of the engines which may last out the journey back to Chungking.

The journey here from Lanchow has been mostly desert. This is part of the Little Gobi, and I am glad we didn't break down in it. Most of the last four days it was just like being on the sea with nothing in sight in all directions, except the snow-mountains of Tibet on the left. The other

Local transport in the Gobi Desert

two trucks of the convoy are usually in sight. Sometimes when they are 5 or 10 miles away they are too small to see, but you can see their white dust trails looking just like two aircraft vapour trails.

The desert isn't all like this. There are parts with great sand dunes, and caravans of camels being led along the sky line in conventional manner.

I have been doing some cooking. The last night before we got in here was particularly pleasant. We stopped at a little oasis like an island in the sea, with a well, and trees, flowers and butterflies. We have eggs, butter, honey, and lots of tinned stuff, so do fairly well. There were a number of those ox carts they have on the Gobi with enormous wheels about 7 feet diameter.

(continued at Lanchow 14th June 1945)

We spent about a week at Suchow, repaired my engine, and bought the petrol. We had a quick journey back here, quite a lot of fresh snow had fallen on the mountains, but the Wu Sa Ling Pass, 9600 feet, was still clear when we came over it. The mountains you can see in Tibet from Suchow are a wonderful sight, there is a great range of 20,000 ft. peaks. I don't know the actual heights of the summits, but my map marks the pass near there as being 18,123 feet. You see a number of Tibetans in the town, I suppose they come over that way.

When we got into Lanchow we were disappointed to find that the missionary to whom our mail is sent had mistakenly forwarded several packets to Suchow. As it goes by mule, and takes a month each way, it was not a very clever idea. However another packet arrived yesterday with your letter of 18th May, the day we first arrived in Lanchow.

I wish I could have seen you papering your room, and getting covered with paste. It is good to think of you in summer frocks and getting sun-burnt (but perhaps ingrained dirt!)

I expect next time I write will be from Shuang Shi Pu, or perhaps Chungking.

yours

John

Letter No. 34: harvest time

4, Cheng Yang Kai
Chungking.
22nd June 1945

Written at Shung Shi Pu (Feng)

My Dear Jean,

We are well on our way back now, and if nothing more goes wrong may be back in Chungking in 8-10 days.

On our last day in Lanchow I happened to meet a meteorologist who told me that the maximum temperature that day was 103 degrees. It didn't feel nearly as hot as some days, so it is just as well we don't carry a thermometer.

We have now got a baby chipmunk which we carry in a truck. This is a delightful thing, I wish you could see it. It is something between a mouse and a squirrel, and has stripes on its sides. It seems to eat anything, a usual day's meal consisting of fried egg, cucumber, rice, dou fu (bean curd), and anything else it can pick up. It sits up like a squirrel and eats its food holding it with both hands.

We have been getting along quite fast, but had some excitement a few days ago when a front wheel came off my truck. We were right up on a mountain ridge, but fortunately were on a straight piece of road, so didn't go over the edge. The axle had broken right through, and several other things were broken. However I managed to fix it with some spares so we could go on in about four hours. It was just as well, as it would not have been a safe place to be in at night!

We are getting down into country areas where things grow, and it is good to see trees and bushes and fields of wheat. The wheat is being harvested and we see people threshing it with flails, and oxen walking round in circles. Yesterday we came into this for the first time, and you could smell the vegetation. I picked a bunch of huge wild strawberries and stuck them in the open windscreen, so we could smell strawberries instead of engine-oil for a change. There were hundreds of butterflies, and I recognized about 15 species I have seen in England.

I hope I shall pick up some mail from you eventually, I expect there will be some at Chungking,

yours,

John

Letter No. 35: back in the capital

Chungking.
2nd July 1945

My Dear Jean,

We are now back in Chungking, and I think we were the fastest Suchow Convoy on record.

It is very hot here, the temperature today is 108°, and I'm afraid I'm too hot to write very much.

I was glad to find two letters from you waiting for me when I got back. It is all very exciting to hear news of demobilisation. I wonder if you will still be at the farm when I get back. I should think it is a much more satisfying job than office work.

I am supposed to be starting some leave next week, but haven't got anything fixed up yet with the Gliding people.

After that I have got a job which should be quite interesting. This is to start a kind of mobile 'garage' in a truck in S.E. Kweichow where we have 20 trucks doing U.N.R.R.A. famine relief work. I expect to fit this truck up with some machinery and tools and to move around wherever the centre of operations happens to be. I shall fit a bed in somewhere, but don't know about a library and a gramophone!

yours

John

Letter No. 36: a Chinese glider pilot

c/o Postal Commissioner,
Kunming.
15th July 1945

My Dear Jean,

I am now in Kunming, having flown down from Chungking yesterday morning. It is good to get into a reasonable climate once more.

Last week-end I had a very pleasant time with the Gliding people at Bei-Pei, about 50 Km. from Chungking.

They looked after me very well, we had two feasts, ate innumerable water-melons, swam in the river, visited the University, and I flew their high-performance 'Rhönsperber' sailplane from the Dragon Mountain, 1100 feet above the landing ground. I only flew for about ten minutes, but it was fine to be flying myself again after so long. I was presented with Chinese glider pilots wings, a photograph was taken, and there were four columns in the Chinese newspaper next day!

Just having landed the Rhönsperber glider on a sand bank at the edge of the Yangtse. The Dragon Mountain can be seen in the background.

The rest of my leave is not fixed up, but I hope to spend a week or two by the Lake here, and then go to work at Kutsing for a bit.

We have got a fine new house to live in at Kunming instead of the old house. It looks just like an English house in the country, and has armchairs, books, and even a refrigerator! I suppose it will soon turn into the usual pigsty F.A.U. members always make of a place in which they live, but at present it is all right.

yours

John

Letter No. 37: idyllic days at the lakeside

> Kutsing,
> Yunnan,
> Free China
> 28th July 1945

My Dear Jean,

Since I wrote last, I have been having a delightfully lazy week. I have been staying in West Jade Village near the Kunming Lake, the place where I was in January. The weather has been fine, and I have been dividing my time between eating, sleeping, sun-bathing and swimming. I have even been too lazy to read or write letters, even to you.

I am sorry to think of you working hard while I am having a time like this, but I shall have to get back to work at Kutsing eventually. I hope we may have a holiday like this some time together and I shan't really complain if it isn't in China.

There are many more flowers out here now than there were in January, and numbers of enormous butterflies. I have seen about 20 kinds new to me - some of them must be 5 or 6 inches wing span.

The place where I swim in the lake is about 2 minutes walk. You go across a small farm-yard (but absolutely nothing like the Barton), through a small bamboo grove and then past about half-a-dozen palm trees beside the path through the paddy fields.

It is the rainy season now, and although it is mostly fine, we sometimes

Afternoon on Lake Kunming

get a thunderstorm about 6 or 7 or in the evening. We have a lot of ducks here, who have nearly all died of some disease, and still keep on dying. It is one of the sights of the place to see 'a dying duck in a thunderstorm'.

There is a gramophone here, but there are few interesting records. However, I went out to see a private film show near here a few days ago and saw a newsreel of Roosevelt's funeral, with almost the whole of the 2nd movement of the Eroica played as background music.

Yesterday we heard the news of the Election results, which sounds very interesting. I was glad to hear Churchill is out, I was afraid people might be foolish enough to keep him on in the peace.

As well as the dying ducks, there seem to be a large number of other fauna here. We don't actually have many water buffaloes, although I saw three in a 'wallow' yesterday near the gate, with just their noses sticking out. There are three dogs and a horrible kitten which squeaks all the time. There are a few hens - two nights ago I thought the rats in my room were making more noise than usual and shone my torch under the bed to see a couple of hens roosting there.

The two servants are not ordinary Chinese, but tribes-people from the hill country. I think they are Miao's. The bigger one is usually known as Frankenstein, the smaller is Hsiao T'ao (Little Peach). I shouldn't think he has ever washed himself or combed his hair, but he doesn't look Chinese.

Time to eat lunch now, - then sleep till tea-time, - cakes today.

yours

John

Letter No. 38: back to the garage routine

Kutsing,
Yunnan.
Free China
9th August 1945

My Dear Jean,

Yesterday was a great day when I received no less than eight letters, including one from you.

I am back in Kutsing, with another two days of leave to run, and am amusing myself by practising Chinese as on the cover of this letter.

I have not let you know about a possible return to England next year, as it was not certain. Working on the same basis of age and length of service as the Armed Forces, my number is 29, which should be demobilised about the end of this year. I hoped to be back by about June, to get a teaching job in September. However news has come recently which is not so cheerful, in that COs will not be demobilised with their counterparts in the Forces, but may have to wait until the end of the War. Anyhow, no one really knows! It makes it more exciting. If I am still not demobilised when my 3 years here are up, perhaps I could do land work with you and help you dig potatoes! Teachers must be urgently needed, so I hope for the best.

For a few days I was expecting to be seeing you again in six months time, and I realise that this is the chief reason why I feel a bit depressed about the news.

Although during the past few unsettled years we didn't meet nearly often enough, I feel that you are my oldest and closest friend, and think about you here rather a lot.

I have done a number of jobs, and met a great many people who I have lost touch with or who have been killed, but you have always been there just the same. I hope you always will be!

Last night we had a bit of a disturbance. A crowd of Chinese soldiers were brought in who had been in a truck accident. Some were very badly hurt. As a transport worker it was a change to be sterilising surgical instruments in a billy-can over a stove, and assisting one of our surgeons at a brain operation, by the light of torches on the common-room floor. We finished at 2.30 a.m. this morning, and the four worst fractured skull cases are still alive.

Next week I shall be back in the Garage again, nearly everyone is ill, so I shall have to be Manager, Asst. Manager, Secretary, and Chief Mechanic!

yours ever

John

Letter No. 39: living rough on the job

Kutsing
19th August 1945

My Dear Jean,

I have just written a letter in Chinese to some friends in England in order to annoy them, but perhaps you would rather I wrote in English as usual. At least the writing and grammar should be a little better.

There is very little to write about this week, as I have been back at work and am at present garage manager here. This means that I live up in the garage instead of at the Hostel about 300 yards away. I have a little attic above the offices, with big windows at one end overlooking the Highway and you can see across the paddy fields to the 'Delectable Mountains'.

I have a bed in one corner, and a stove by the window. In the mornings Hsiao Yang (the more intelligent looking of the workers) cooks my breakfast while I am shaving and dressing. This consists of eggs and ham. The ham comes from Suamwei, and is the best I have ever tasted - very strong!

I was interested to hear you have a boy from Bethnal Green with you at the farm. I wonder if he has ever been to the Hospital there. I used to wheel victims from the boys' ward (D.5.) down to the operating theatre fairly often.

The war against Japan we are told is over now. We are having excitements of a slightly different kind.

I wonder if regulations about sending photos have been relaxed now. If so, another real photo of you would gladden me a lot. I only have the airgraph one (not very well reproduced) and two small polyphoto prints. Wouldn't it be awful if I forgot what you look like, and didn't recognise you when we meet again! I wonder where or when that will be, perhaps at Honiton Station again sometime next year. You will be able to recognise me from my long white hair and anxious expression, also habit of swearing in Chinese.

yours ever,

John

Letter No. 40: another Great Feast

Kutsing,
Yunnan.
China
26th August 1945

My Dear Jean,

The biggest event of this week was our Feast at a place in the town. This was for transport employees and members, and about 50 people attended. Not including drinks, it only cost $416,000.

It was a good meal, and consisted of 19 dishes. I didn't know what most of them were, but two of the more exciting ones were identified as cuttle fish and clams.

The next morning we had an enormous group photograph taken at the garage. I saw a proof this morning, and it has come out quite well, except for a dog which was moving and has come out a shapeless blur.

Garage workforce

Did I tell you the Gliding people sent me photos taken at Bei-Pei, with a letter written in rather peculiar English. I replied in a letter written in rather peculiar Chinese! Their letter had a quotation from Confucius in it, perhaps I should have quoted from Shakespeare, or perhaps the Bible in my reply.

Our trucks are managing to get through again at present, after last week's trouble, and one arrived last night, breaking its connecting rod as it came in through the gateway.

I have just been rereading 'Murder in the Cathedral' by T.S. Eliot. I still think it is very fine. I seem to remember that you once told me that you liked it.

We have had a member with us now who was training to be a full-time pianist. Last night he played a lot of Bach and finished up with a 'boogie-woogie' version of 'God Save the King' and 'San Min Chu I'. Someone gave him a little theme from Debussy and he played on it for about ten minutes in all sorts of different styles.

Last night I dreamt about you again, and was very fed up when I woke up and found you weren't there. I can't decide whether this is a

Good Thing, or a Bad Thing!

yours ever,

John

Letter No. 41: thoughts of Devon

> Kutsing,
> Yunnan,
> China.
> 2/9/45

My Dear Jean,

Thanks for two air-letters which arrived on Friday.

I was glad to hear you had got out to Seaton in a car, and later on to Sidmouth again. It was a pity you couldn't bathe, but I suppose the coast will be available everywhere for this soon. I can't think when I last swam in the sea, it was probably with you at Torquay, unless you count Bombay, which was really only a pool attached to the sea. However, I still know how to swim, as I was in the river a few miles from here last weekend. I don't suppose I shall ever be further from the sea than I was at Suchow, in Kansu.

Yes, I wish I could have been with you there too. Things are still very vague here, but I think there's little doubt that we shall be bathing together on the Devon coast under a year from now.

The rainy season really is nearly over now, and we only get an occasional afternoon thunderstorm. It is a wonderful day today, and I hope to get out somewhere this afternoon.

One of our new members is a typewriter expert, and has just overhauled one of our garage typewriters. We don't often get one going as well as this (also with new ribbon) so I have used it to address the envelope. We don't have Chinese typewriters, so I have to do that part by hand as usual!

yours ever,

John

Letter No. 42: music from the railway

Kutsing,
Yunnan,
China.
9th Sep. 1945

My Dear Jean,

Thanks for your letter of 19th August. I'm sorry you haven't been hearing from me very regularly, please let me know if any of the numbered series are missing. Just now I am leading a fairly regular life, spending each night at the same place, so it is easier to write regularly.

The rainy season is getting less and less evident, and last week-end I went out swimming in the River with the Cook and Shu Ben Tsay, a boy of about 13 who now works at the garage and cooks my breakfast there. It was a fine place, among the hills, just above a small weir, about two miles from here.

I hope to go out there again tomorrow afternoon with some of our Chinese mechanics if the weather is fine.

Kutsing railway station

The man at the railway level-crossing sentry box just outside my window has now got a new pipe. It sounds just like a recorder, he plays various Chinese tunes on it, and has almost encouraged me to get my own recorder out from its box beneath my bed where it is still mouldering.

The train this morning had only five passengers riding on the front of the engine, but it made up for this by towing a little plate-layers trolley on a rope behind the last carriage.

I heard from the London Gliding Club again the other day. Flying is still prohibited, but they have ordered two new two-seaters.

yours ever,

John

Chapter 6

Letters to Jean - thoughts of home

The autumn of 1945 saw me back in Kutsing, busy looking after the workforce and the trucks. The great world conflict was now over, but the Chinese revolution was just beginning. Naturally the thoughts of most Westerners were focused on resuming normal life back home. Demobilisation became a possibility rather earlier than expected, and the F.A.U. agreed to release me in January 1946. After a farewell feast, I was soon on my way to Calcutta where there were serious riots. While waiting for a troopship home from India I tried to beat the legendary F.A.U. hitch-hiking record, from London to Oxford, accompanied by a grand piano. I light-heartedley accepted a hitch-hike to Rangoon and Bangkok with an R.A.F. officer who made regular 1,000-mile round-trips for food delicacies for the officers' mess. But I caught the boat to Glasgow, and after a final journey to Torquay, my Chinese odyssey came to its natural and appropriate end.

Letter No. 43: new plans from Chungking?

Kutsing,
China.
16th September 1945

My Dear Jean,

Another week of confused rumours, some F.A.U. members are going up to Honan* to investigate large scale work there. The work with U.N.R.R.A. in Kwangsi seems to be closing down owing to the impossible position between rival political rackets, each side of which blocks the other from getting anything done!

We have our Staff Meeting at Chungking next week where representatives from each Section meet and talk for 25 hours a day for a week. Perhaps they will get something decided.

Anyway my knowledge of the geography of China is still increasing, and I expect yours is also at second hand.

This week has passed with no events outside the garage, and somehow burnt-out clutches, punctures and broken springs don't sound as interesting as hay-making and harvesting. I haven't even got as far as Sidmouth on a bicycle. Although of course if you were so foolish as to go outside the compound after dark you might have something to write about!

Prices are falling rapidly now, and the cost of rice has about halved here during the past three weeks. We shall soon have to be using notes smaller than $100 - at present we use mostly $1,000 notes. Even these make quite a packet when you have to pay $416,000 for a feast, as I did three weeks ago.

yours ever,

John

*Not to be confused with Hunan. The provinces are mostly in pairs like this just to make it more difficult.

Letter No. 44: new trucks from India

> Kutsing,
> Yunnan,
> China.
> 23rd Sep 1945,

My Dear Jean,

I have just got another ration of Air Letter Forms. These are a very poor quality, I suppose they must have been made in India.

Thanks for your letter of 25th August.

The overturning of your lorry sounds quite like life here. Except that when they overturn they often roll 500 or 1000 feet down a hillside, and take much more than an hour to get back on to the road again. We have got ten more new trucks in Kunming. Only unfortunately they have been driven in (new) from India by Chinese Drivers, and look in a worse condition that the oldest of ours over the last four years! Perhaps the engines have not been ruined forever.

I thought that the rainy season really was over, with perfect weather every day, but today is overcast and drizzling, exactly like an English summer day! So we have mud again instead of dust.

The American member who was working here has now left, and I have a New Zealander as my assistant, which is a very great improvement.

Staff Meeting should be nearly over now and in a few weeks time letters should arrive from Chungking (if they're not lost) to tell us what exciting schemes are being hatched for our future.

A spider has just made a web between two of my socks which I have hung up outside the window to dry, but at this rate they won't be dry today!

yours ever,

John

Letter No. 45: garage payroll in millions

Kutsing,
Yunnan,
China.
23rd Sept. 1946

My Dear Jean,

I meant to write to you yesterday, but I have been in bed for a couple of days. I have been feeling a bit poor for a few days, on Friday I borrowed a thermometer, found my temperature was 101°, went to bed and immediately felt better than for weeks! However, I am now up again, and feel fine.

I had two letters from you last week, written on 3rd and 9th September. I note that you are 27, an awful age isn't it? But you'll never be able to catch me up, and I hope you'll always really be just the same. Ten stone is just about half the weight of my sailplane, and that never feels to weigh anything at all, at any rate when it's in the air.

You will be glad to hear that my mouth watered all over the place in reading about your Goose, Roast Potatoes, Yorkshire Pudding, Blackberry and Apple Pie and Cream. Don't eat too much.

I'm glad to hear you are going to investigate sending me some more photos of yourself. I think the censorship is closing down soon, and I don't see how they can object anyway. If they are very like you, I imagine the censor might keep them for himself!

I seem to have plenty of work to do here now. It made me feel quite a big executive to find out last week that my total employees' payroll is as much as $3,460,000. I now have two telephones on my desk to give me 'face', one is connected with the Machine Shop, and the other one doesn't go anywhere at all.

I'm sorry to hear the knees of your stockings get worn out at your window writing to me. I don't think the proprieties would be upset by your sometimes writing in bare legs if necessary! No silk stockings yet I suppose?

Goodbye for now,

yours ever,

John

Letter No. 46: cut off from Kunming

> Kutsing,
> Yunnan,
> China.
> 8th October 1945

My Dear Jean,

Owing to events which have possibly reached your newspapers, we are cut off from Kunming, and are receiving no mail. So I haven't heard from you for a bit, also I wonder if this letter will get through. I have got a pass from the military allowing me to walk on the street, and things are quiet here now.

We can get the other way - towards Kweichow, and yesterday I took a day off from the Garage to drive 70 Km. to Pingyi to buy coke. I took our old Diesel truck, which I have had renovated. This looks very old, but has a tremendously powerful (and noisy) engine. It sounds and feels just like an aeroplane.

Various things fell off the truck and went wrong. It took four hours to buy and load the coke, and by the time we finished it was dark. So we had to stay there for the night.

I slept in the cab. I have been sleeping in a bed (of sorts) for two months now, and found it a little uncomfortable in the cab at first - getting tied up round the steering wheel. However, I soon got sorted out and when I woke up this morning I felt as if I was stretched out straight.

We (Wilf Howarth - Canadian Asst. Garage Manager and myself) have got our room above the garage straightened out now. This afternoon it is cold, (it was cold and drizzling in the mountains this morning), so I have got a little charcoal fire and have just been making tea and toast. As usual I wish you were here to share it, or better still to make it for me!

yours ever,

John

Letter No. 47: offers of gliding and farming

Kutsing,
Yunnan,
China.
14th October 1945

My Dear Jean,

The Trouble seems to be nearly over now, and a great packet of mail managed to get through on Thursday, the first for a long time. This had two letters from you in it, which was a Good Thing.

The ban on sending photographs into China must have been lifted by now, as the censorship on mail into China has ceased (at any rate officially!). So I hope you will be able to send me one or more different ones to cheer me up. Address these direct to Kutsing, air mail.

My job now is quite interesting and almost worthwhile, but I am still trying to make arrangements to get back early next year (probably not until March or April). Clayesmore might be able to get me released to teach there, which would have the great advantage of being near you, but I don't want to return there permanently. The Cambridge Gliding Club still thinks it might be able to give me a job, which is rather too far away. (You have an aerodrome near, I suppose I might be able to fly down there). My friends the Slazengers are getting a farm near Cambridge and have offered me a job there. I am not really very keen on farm work, but if I am going to do land work I hope I could do it with you.

So things are still rather vague, and anyway, no-one knows anything about the release of COs.

I'm afraid there isn't much news in this letter. Work was as usual this week, except that we received some new tinned rations, including luxuries like butter, jam, grapefruit juice and cocoa.

The real news I had probably better not put in a letter.

yours ever

John

Letter No. 48: more trucks than ever

Kutsing,
Yunnan,
China.
20/10/45

My Dear Jean,

Thanks for your letter of 29th Sep. and also for the one written in the train, which arrived this afternoon. You can see quite clearly in this the point at which the lights came on!

I find myself doing much the same thing now myself, but not in a train. I must go and start our Diesel engine which works the lights.

It's on now, but I don't suppose you notice any difference, except perhaps that my hand is less steady after cranking the engine.

I do hope you have enjoyed the rest of your holiday, and the weather has kept good. I like to hear about the sea, as I am a very long way away from it, even in Kutsing. The nearest is Haiphong, about 400 miles away, but as there is no means of getting there, it seems much further!

There is nothing much to write about this week, as we have been very busy. Just now I have 18 trucks (lorries to you?) in my yard, which was originally designed for about four or five. If I want to move any around from one place to another it needs careful working out like a game of chess, usually including backing two or three out into the Road. On Thursday we backed one out with a boy in the cab to watch it, and forgot all about it until lunch-time!

We are sending off our mobile workshop tomorrow. I have had a new workshop fitted up here, and the truck is going to our new work in Honan (not Hunan). If you have a map you may find Chengchow, at the meet of the Pekin-Hankow Railway and the one from Sian.

No-one quite seems to know what they are going to do there, and it will be interesting to see what turns out.

yours ever,

John

Letter No. 49: life getting quite luxurious

> Kutsing,
> Yunnan,
> China.
> 4/11/45.

My Dear Jean,

I usually like to write to you on Sundays, but last week-end, with one thing and another, I didn't get a free moment. A number of the garage employees had a fight with hammers and pokers, and some trucks came in, so I was as busy as on a week-day.

The local truck (100 mile radius) came in yesterday with 11 people on board from Kunming. Several were people I hadn't seen for nearly a year, and there were three new arrivals who flew into China two days before.

Life is getting more and more luxurious here just now, and we have a good deal of tinned stuff to eat. This morning we had bacon and eggs (2), grapefruit juice, toast, butter and jam. So you're not the only one who can write about food!

However, I can't say that I have seen any Wall's Ice Cream men around Kutsing recently. I was glad to hear about the choc-bars.

A letter of yours has just arrived dated 27th May. It came from Lanchow and appears to be one of the ones diverted by the helpful missionary. At the end you ask about little bits of Chinese at the end of my letters. I don't remember which they were - they might have been 'ping an' which means 'level peace' or 'good wishes' or perhaps 'tso ni kuay lor', a conventional sort of 'yours truly' ending, literally 'invoke you speedy happiness'. The same character , when pronounced 'yueh' means 'music'.

It's rather a fine character, almost as fine as the one below, which you see on notices by the road, and means 'hairpin bend'.

Yours

John

Letter No. 50: Beethoven bringing the house down

> Kutsing,
> Yunnan
> 11th Nov. 1945

My Dear Jean,

Thanks for your letter of 21st October. I was interested to hear about the Gliding Book with a description of my Dunstable-Cambridge flight in it. I don't know who has written this, possibly Dr. Slater, but I hope to have a copy of it one day.

We have got a lot of salvage here recently, including some photographic materials, so I should be able to do some printing of my photographs at last. I can't see that anyone can find any excuse to suppress them from being posted in peacetime, particularly as they will mostly be ones showing some of the fine scenery in this country! Photos may now be sent <u>into</u> China, and the same applies to news.

I may get time to do some this week and will send you some as soon as I can. The only photos I have taken myself were with the camera I was issued for the Suchow Convoy, but I can probably get the use of other people's negatives for some enlargements.

We have also got a radio-gramophone, in fact life is getting quite luxurious! It is very large and powerful (it is actually out of a cinema!) and last night I played the 5th Symphony and brought down several pieces of ceiling.

I went out for a walk today, over the local hill, and swam across the river and came back via the other side. It was a glorious day, and all the people are out in the fields harvesting the rice, and threshing the grain with flails in their yards.

Thrashing grain at Kutsing

Tomorrow is a holiday, Sun Yat Sen's Birthday, and I hope to get out again, possibly with a camera this time.

yours ever,

John

Letter No. 51: a new photograph

Kutsing,
Yunnan.
18th Nov. 1945

My Dear Jean,

I was very glad to get your letter of 3rd November with a photograph of you, I hope this will not be the last. Although it is quite small, it is easy to tell at a glance which is you and which is the cow!

Jean, the land-girl

Now photographs seem to be getting through, may I return the compliment by sending you some? There is a sinister one taken in Kunming last year for my driving licence. The other three are fairly self-explanatory. I'm afraid they are rather scratched, as a result of letting someone else develop them for me. Your Air Mail Letter did the journey in 14 days, arriving only a day after the Air Letter posted 5 days earlier.

I was interested to hear that you may be released from the Land Army in January if you want to go, and hope you will let me know what developments occur. I'm afraid my first selfish reactions on hearing this were to hope that when I return you will be at a job where I can come and see you and you will have some time off for us to be together. Anyway, England isn't very large, and wherever you are, I shan't be further from you than the distance from here to our next garage, and even if I haven't any money I can always hitch-hike!

I still don't know what I shall be doing, and am still waiting for an official letter offering me the job as instructor to the Cambridge Gliding Club. If this comes off, it will be a pleasant way of getting used to England again, and to fill in until September when I hope to get a new teaching job. I don't think it's much good going back to Clayesmore, as the same headmaster is virtually in control as 'Warden' and the Officers Training Corps is now compulsory for all boys except those in the bottom form.

If you ever have any spare time with nothing to do, (!?!), how about studying Chinese Cookery? It would be wonderful if you could cook food such as we have here, but perhaps you don't like it yourself.

Goodbye for now,

yours ever,

John

Letter No. 52: civil war in the North

> Kutsing,
> Yunnan,
> China.
> 25/11/45.

My Dear Jean,

We have got a batch of a different sort of Air Letter Forms, and I am trying one out to see how quick it is. As these have Indian stamps, they have to be sent to our India Office in a big packet all together. Anyway, the paper is much better to write on.

The weather is still as glorious as ever, and convoys of 5 trucks keep on rolling in. We were very lucky this week, as each time I sent a convoy off (twice) another one arrived in here on the same day.

I am writing this on a Sunday morning for a change. I have just been down to our Hostel for the Sunday breakfast, and when I have finished this I am going out for a day's walk with one or two others.

We have got an F.A.U. 'Jeep' here at last, and I have just been painting our insignia on it. When it arrived it had painted on it, literally, 'Middle Flowery People's Kingdom Red Ten Character Association' or 'Chinese Red Cross' for short. (The Chinese for 'ten' is +).

I don't suppose the Chinese have been able to suppress the fact that there is now widespread civil war in the Northern Provinces. In case you get bits of news every now and then, you may be glad to hear that at present it is quiet down here, and the Fascist v. Communist war in the North is not likely to spread down here.

Hoping to get some photographs ready for you in the next week.

yours ever,

John

Letter No. 53: Our War is spreading

Kutsing,
Yunnan.
China
2nd December 1945

My Dear Jean,

Since I wrote last week, winter seems to have come. Instead of going about in shorts, I am wearing battle-dress, and a big overcoat and fur hat when I go outside. I hope it's only temporary.

Last Sunday I went out with a friend and his camera with a telephoto lens, which he used for photographing small birds on the other side of the river. It was too hot to go very far, and I swam in the river again (? perhaps for the last time this year).

I'm afraid the war here is spreading, but nothing is happening yet in Yunnan. We get very little news, and that mostly from foreign newspapers!

I hope the photographs I sent you a fortnight ago have reached you by now, and that at least one more is on the way from you!

We have been very busy this week, and I just managed to get our 61 employees' wages worked out and paid by the 1st of the month. I had to carry the money up here in a rucksack. 2 million dollars is quite a weight, even if it is in $500 notes!

The next thing is to balance the accounts. I have always had difficulty in doing this even with small amounts of English money. With a total something like $5,647,893 I shall be lucky if I get within 100,000 of the correct total.

We have got a new vehicle in here now. It is a Ford V8 with a small truck body and is very fast and powerful. It gives me considerable status, although I have had to engage coolies to push it for starting.

yours ever,

John

Letter No. 54: trouble with government troops

Kutsing,
Yunnan,
8th December 1945

My Dear Jean,

Thank you for an Air Letter and Air Mail Letter of 23rd Nov. The latter arrived today, after 16 days, but the former took 22 days. However, both vary enormously.

I was interested to hear you have decided to return to the Prudential. I suppose that means you will be returning to London eventually. It will be a pity to leave farm work, but I suppose there isn't much doubt that that is what you will have to do. It will be good to have more time off again, and I am glad that it will make it easier for me to see you when I get back. I hope if they want to move you, it will still be somewhere in the S. or S.W.

If the Bill for release of COs goes through Parliament as it is now, my number might go down to 26, as they propose to count time from the tribunal, and not when 'directed' work was started.

We have got several hundred new records from the departing Americans, including most of the Beethoven Symphonies. Also I have just listened to a very fine recording by Toscanini of the 3rd Piano Concerto. We have 'In a Summer Garden', I think the only Delius record here.

We have had more trouble with the Chinese Army this week. Several soldiers* rifled one of our trucks and tried to shoot the driver. I spent all yesterday dashing around complaining to people, finishing with a three hour interview with the Local General (all in Chinese!) Members here are now taking bets as to whether I shall 'be promoted to Chungking, or go mad and eat my young' (whatever that may mean!)

The weather is now behaving itself again, and I am thinking about a swim in the river again tomorrow.

yours ever,

John

* 'Government' troops.

Letter No. 55: picnic with the boys

Kutsing,
Yunnan,
China.
16/12/45.

My Dear Jean,

I am sending you three more photographs, and hope they will get through.

One is the Pagoda at Kunming, the open street scene is Weining, and the close-up one is at Kutsing. I hope they will reach you all right.

Pagoda at Kunming

Picnic with the boys

Things go on much the same here, with the usual crises - lack of spare parts and drivers. The weather is still good, and I went out for a pleasant picnic today with Shu Pen Tsai (a boy of about 13 who works here) and three friends of his. We went a couple of miles up the river and had a swim, complicated by an inner tube one of them had brought along. We had an enormous lunch of American tinned food, and then I wanted to go to sleep. However, the boys wouldn't even sit down, but rushed around throwing flat stones to skim on the water-surface.

The ground is all getting drier now, and the hill at the back is a lovely chocolate colour.

yours ever,

John

Letter No. 56: demob not far away

> Kutsing,
> Yunnan,
> China.
> 30/12/45

My Dear Jean,

I'm sorry I wasn't able to write a letter as usual to you last week-end, as I have been in bed with a recurrence of malaria - temperature jumping about from 99° to 102°.

Thanks for two letters, one to Chungking, and one to Kutsing. The Kutsing one was about 3 days quicker.

You had better use up your air-letter forms quickly now, as I am hoping to leave China very soon. I have written asking if I can leave in the next two weeks, but haven't heard yet. So I hope I shall have left by the time you get this letter, but I can't quite believe that it will really happen.

The reason is that I find my demobilisation is sooner than I thought, and also I have a job for 1946 at any rate - Chief Instructor to the Cambridge Gliding Club, to start as soon after 1st Feb. as possible!

I don't think there's much chance I shall be back before March unless I can arrange to fly.

I am only thinking of this job as temporary, as it is a long way away from you, and also I really want to go back to teaching.

There are rumours that the air service to India has been stopped. If so I shall have to fly to Shanghai, and get a boat from there, which will take a very long time.

I suppose by now you are back at the Prudential, and hope you aren't finding it too much of a strain.

Do you know if there's any chance of your all moving back to London?

yours ever,

John

Letter No. 57: farewell to Kutsing

Kutsing,
Yunnan,
China.
6/1/46

My Dear Jean,

Thanks for your letter of 14th Dec. which arrived three days ago. I enclose two more photographs, one a rather sinister one of myself eating out of an American ration can in a temple, and the other of people threshing the rice in a field near the river here. As you see, this work is all done by women!

I am leaving here tomorrow by Unit truck for Chungking, to explain to the Council why I want to leave. I hope they will let me go in a few week's time, I should probably be able to fly direct from Chungking to India.

Last night they gave me a sort of farewell supper here, and presented me with a pair of Chinese scrolls. These are rather amusing, with both characters and pictures of my activities in China. I hope to show them to you soon!

I will write when I get to Chungking, and let you know how things are going.

yours ever,

John

Letter No. 58: rough ride out of China

Calcutta
India
23rd Jan. 1946

My Dear Jean,

I am out of China now, and am writing this letter in Calcutta. I expect

I shall have to wait at least a month here for a ship, and should then be back in three or four weeks.

It was a long day yesterday. I left Cheng Yang Kai at 5.30 a.m. and arrived at Upper Wood Street at 11.20 p.m. I had to wait 5 hours (time to have lunch and travel from London to Torquay!) on the Chungking air-field, and then had a total of nearly 10 hours flying time. The first 3 hours to Kunming was very rough, and I was horribly sick.

Long distance air-travel seems even more unreal than any other kind. I left Chungking after five hours arguing with Chinese on a damp November-like foggy morning, - landed in Kunming about lunch-time in a windy March-like day, with storms and low cloud - came down over the jungle to Bhamo in a perfect calm tropical evening, among palm trees and temples by the Irrawaddy. I felt rather a fool there when I stepped down to the ground in my battle-dress and heavy khaki overcoat. These had been suitable for Kunming, but at Bhamo people wore sun-helmets and shorts.

We went on as the sun was setting and after another 3½ hours saw the lights of Calcutta, and did the first night landing I have ever experienced.

Things are quite incredibly different here, everything is clean and efficient. The registration and customs was all over in ten minutes instead of the 2½ hours excited inefficiency of Chungking.

It is quite hot here, but not too bad, and it is quite cool enough to sleep at night.

Hoping to hear soon what you are doing.

yours ever,

John

Letter No. 59: hanging around in Calcutta

Calcutta
India.
3rd Feb. 1946.

My Dear Jean,

Thanks for your letter of 19th Jan. which reached me very quickly considering the fact that it went to Chungking first.

It is not so good to think of you back working in an office again, I hope you don't find it too bad after the farm work. You will at least have more free time, but I don't think this really makes up for a job you don't care for.

There is no news so far of my getting on a boat to England. I have been here nearly a fortnight, and I suppose I may have to wait another month or more.

It is rather horrible hanging around with nothing to do. I can't go off on a job or on a holiday to Darjeeling in case news suddenly comes through of my ship.

I have found a very good bookshop, which helps a little. I have seen a new Smythe book and bought a few of various kinds. There are also many cinemas, but they don't have any films on I have ever heard of, which I suppose is not so very unlikely.

The Calcutta Symphony Orchestra is playing a concert next Sunday including Beethoven's 8th Symphony. It will be interesting to see how this goes.

The weather is a little warmer, and the maximum yesterday was 89°, which is quite enough for me.

Last night we went to the station to see some friends off to Bombay in an air-conditioned 1st class carriage for their three days journey. On the way back at about 10.30 p.m. we all called in to an ice cream shop and ordered the most expensive kind (about 2s 6d in English money!)

yours ever,

John

Letter No. 60: hitchhike to Rangoon and Bangkok

No 1, Upper Wood Street
Calcutta.
India
14th Feb. 1946

My Dear Jean,

You may be surprised to hear that I am not writing this in Calcutta, but at Hmawbi*, a little village about 30 miles from Rangoon.

Last week I met an R.A.F. pilot in Air Transport Command who offered me a lift down here. I still had no news of my boat and was very tired of Calcutta so was glad of a change. We had trouble getting to the airfield owing to the rioting which was just starting. This has been rather bad, and is still going on.

* Pronounced 'More-bee'.

We left Calcutta at about 11 oc at night, and had a pleasant 4-hour journey in brilliant moonlight. The coastline of the 'Mouths' of the Ganges was a very fine sight.

Yesterday I had a look round Rangoon, which is of course a bit bomb-damaged, but seems quite a pleasant town.

Tomorrow I hope to continue my tour of the Capitals of the World by a trip to Bangkok, the capital of Thailand, which everyone here seems to think is a fine place.

I am living in a tent here, and have been eating in the Officers Mess. Just here there isn't much to see, except jungle, which begins about 20 yards from where I am sitting. This morning I went in a jeep to the village, which is on the Road which eventually reaches China. Burmese villages seem rather like Chinese ones, but the houses are all made of a darker wood, and the floors are raised a few feet off the ground on stilts. Of course the clothes are different, and everyone wears a kind of skirt. The people look more like Chinese than Indians, but are brown coloured.

The weather is hotter here, and the first storm of the monsoon apparently arrived last week, but there is very little cloud at present.

It will be just too bad if I miss my boat, as no-one is allowed into Calcutta at present, but I hope the fighting will be over soon. Anyway, it's no good worrying about it, and I might as well learn some more geography while I have the chance!

yours ever

John

Letter No. 61: waiting for a boat at Bombay

Taj Mahal Hotel,
Bombay.
Monday 25th Jan 1946.

My Dear Jean,

If everything goes all right I should be getting on a ship tomorrow for the last stage of my journey to the U.K. I shall be on the S.S. Batory which I think is a kind of troopship.

As you have probably been reading in the papers, there is a bit of trouble going on in this country. I left Calcutta on Friday, on what turned out to be the last train to leave, and arrived here yesterday morning. There has been mob rule in this city for some days, and about 300 people have been killed so far. Today it is much quieter, and I ventured out in the streets without seeing any trouble.

This hotel is a very big one, and is very full. Last night I shared a room with two Press Correspondents, a man called Jones of the New York Times and Fisher of the Daily Mail. Tonight a Norwegian has just come in, who incredible as it seems, was in London on Saturday! He said it was cold and windy, and is feeling a bit the worse for wear after having done the journey in three days. It is fairly hot here, going up to over 90° in the middle of the day.

It is very exciting being so near home at last. A lot of our people have been disappointed on return to England, but I know one thing that won't disappoint, and that will be seeing you again. I think about you rather a lot, and it will be wonderful to see you. One thing about being away for two years is that you get a clearer idea of the things that matter and the people that matter in England!

I expect I shall be able to post a letter to you at Aden and perhaps Port Said.

yours ever

John

Letter No. 62: almost there

S.S. Batory
Red Sea,
3rd March 1946.

My Dear Jean,

We have been at sea for about five days now, and this morning turned the corner into the Red Sea. The whole journey is supposed to take about 16 days, and we are going to Glasgow. I shall have a few things to settle up with the F.A.U. in London, and expect it would be best to see you at the week-end when you have more time free. So if all goes well, I hope to arrive at the appropriate railway stn. on the evening of Fri. 22nd.

I shall be handing in this letter at the Ships office, to be posted either at Suez or Port Said, and hope it will arrive before me.

This ship is quite large and there are about 1100 people on board, mostly apparently Army Captains and Colonels with their wives and families. My cabin is not bad as they go, it is above the water line and has a porthole. I share it with four others - an N.F.S. man, a Czech Lieutenant, and two engineers.

It was a bit rough the 2nd day out, and I was very nearly sick. Today it is calmer, but we are rolling quite a lot. The Red Sea is not as hot as it was when I went the other way, but it is very sticky all the same. The food is quite good, which is just as well, as I seem to do little except eat and sleep. I have got sun-burned, and can see the tip of my nose is a horrible reddish-purple colour. I expect by the time I see you it will have all peeled off in horrible patches.

So it looks as if I shall be seeing Scotland at last! I'm afraid I shall be trying to leave it as soon as possible to get to London. Someone told me that they had heard on the radio this morning that there had been big snow storms. I hope they get this cleared up in time.

We have had two cinema shows on board so far - 'Going My Way' with Bing Crosby, and 'They were Sisters'. There are a number of ENSA people on board, and I expect they and others will produce some kind of entertainment.

I have sent off a food parcel from Calcutta which I hope will arrive (or did I tell you about this before?).

yours ever

John

Letter No. 63: Home!

Logandene
Hemel Hempstead
19th March 1946

My Dear Jean,

Thanks for your letter which arrived this morning.

I expect I should be arriving from Clayesmore, so will pick up at Exeter the train which gets to Torquay at 6.15 p.m. on Friday.

Thank you for information about accommodation. Would you please book the cheaper one for Friday, Sat or Sun nights, it would be fine if you can get Sat. and Sun. free.

You may have heard about the 'Batory' being held up for vaccination. However, I got off at last on Sunday night, and got here on Monday evening.

See you Friday,

yrs ever,

John

CHAPTER 7

China Revisited

In December 1946 Jean and I were married at Babbacombe, Devon. We moved to Yorkshire in January 1947 to my teaching job at the Friends School at Great Ayton, and after that we joined another Quaker school, Leighton Park, in Reading where I taught Maths and Physics. Our three children, Janet, Ann and Colin were born there. In the meantime both Jean and I had been accepted as members of the Society of Friends.

After twenty years I moved across the road to the University of Reading to start a new career in scientific research related to gliding and the atmosphere. Five years later I was fortunate enough to be invited to join the Department of Applied Mathematics and Theoretical Physics at the University of Cambridge where I have worked happily ever since.

For many years there seemed little chance of going back to China, and all visits by foreigners were very difficult. However, after I had been working at Cambridge for about ten years, things began to change when Chinese scientists came to Cambridge. And some of them started to work in my Department. Professor George Batchelor, the Head of the Department, made contacts with the Chinese Academy of Sciences and visited China in 1980.

It was impossible in 1981 to get permission to revisit Kutsing and my other haunts in S.W. China, but I was very glad to be invited for a three-week visit, based in Beijing, supported by the Royal Society. I was hosted in China by the rather grandly named "Water Conservancy Hydroelectric River Scientific Research Institute". The interests here were close to my recent experimental work on gravity currents, related to atmospheric convection and the sea breeze. I gave ten lectures on these subjects at Universities and other Institutes, including Beijing, Tientsin, Hangchou, and Shanghai,

Jean came with me, and our friends, Chia Fu and Shen Jing showed us the sights of Beijing. Jean and I were able to go off on our own, and one day as we sat in a Park I was glad to find that my Chinese was still good enough to carry on simple conversations, especially with children. We went shopping, fought our way onto buses and managed to travel on the Underground.

Later we stayed in Hangzhou, which Marco Polo thought was the finest city in the world. I would still mark it pretty high! I had asked if I could view the famous Hangzhou Bore in the Jientang River. With a special visa in my passport, we observed this on the September Full Moon. It was a glorious occasion and hundreds of people had gathered on the river bank to view the passage of the Bore. Everyone seemed to be there, and one of the Hangzhou scientists even met his mother-on-law in the crowd. She had come all the way from Shanghai to see the Bore.

At Shanghai, Jean and I visited the site of the first meeting, in 1921, of the Chinese Communist Party. This was preserved as a kind of "shrine" with parties of schoolchildren queuing to visit. The curator was a real enthusiast! On our trip down the Huang Pu River to its junction with the Yangtse, we met two German glider pilots who were teaching the Chinese to fly gliders. This recalled the occasion nearly forty years previously when I had flown a Rhönsperber, a glider of German design, from the Dragon Mountain near Chungking.

A few days later we made a wonderful journey from Guilin down the Li River, passing hundreds of improbable limestone peaks.

After my return to England there were more Chinese working with us in Cambridge. Perhaps there were only as many as four, but I started a rumour that "in this Department on Fridays every one speaks Chinese". This habit did not become as widespread as I had hoped!

Two years later I managed to persuade the Royal Society to subsidise another visit for me and Jean to China. My purpose was to meet some of the many friends I had made in my previous visit and to spend sixteen days at Beijng, working with Chia Fu in his laboratory at the Institute of Mechanics.

During this time we spent an enjoyable day on a trip by bus to the Purple Bamboo Park with colleagues Mr. Wang and Miss Wu. I enjoyed this as an opportunity to improve my Chinese, and heard afterwards that they had both enjoyed the chance to improve their English.

Before returning to England we went to Xi'an to visit a Chinese scientist who had worked with me in Cambridge. We went by train, and I was particularly pleased to be allowed to do this without the usual compulsory guide or interpreter. Although taking seventeen hours, it was a good journey, and during the night we could hear the wonderful noise of the steam engine in front hauling us up the mountains. Also my Chinese language seemed to work, with the co-operation of the train staff. While we were at Xi'an, we managed to slip in a visit to the recently discovered "terracotta warriors".

Many of the changes I could see in China since my earlier time there, such as the lack of beggars on the street and the disappearance of starving people, have been due to the Communist Revolution. Battles between the Communists and the Kuomintang had been going on at the time I was writing my letters from China. For censorship reasons I was always careful to make no

Crowds gathering to view the Hangzhou Bore (1981)

Strange contours along the Li River (1981)

specific mention of these events, but hints of military action can be detected in several letters. In those days we found that the Communist armies were more sympathetic with the people, and even paid for the food they took and for the damage they did. This was unheard of from the Kuomintang Generals, who did not have a good reputation.

Later on, in the time of the Cultural Revolution in the 1960s, several Chinese scientists I met told me they had to leave their research posts and do agricultural work in the country. During this time I believe the walls of Kutsing were pulled down, presumably in an attempt to drag this charming medieval city into the twentieth century.

During my second post-revolutionary visit to Beijing, I noticed in the Institute of Mechanics that the enormous statue of Mao Tse-tung had disappeared. When I commented on this to my Chinese friends, they said, 'He was a great man, but made some mistakes in his later life'.

On the subject of war and pacifism, my opinions have altered little over the years. At the end of the Great War, there was a general belief that all Germans were subhuman. In later years when I met a few through gliding, I was a little surprised to find how normal they seemed to be.

When I was about twelve in late 1920s, I can remember my parents taking me to see Mahatma Gandhi arriving at Folkestone to negotiate with the British government. My father, who died when I was thirteen, had quite liberal views, and was interested in Gandhi's ideas. At that time, and for about another twenty years, Gandhi was consistently demonised in the British Press, and portrayed as an enemy of Western civilisation. But he persevered with his non-violent methods, and eventually brought about a resolution of the conflict in India at the time of Independence in 1947. Now many regard him not only as a very saintly person, but one of the wisest figures of the twentieth century.

As a pacifist, I believe a little progress was made in the last century. Certainly it is far more acceptable for people to express these views today. I can only see that war leads to war, cruelty causes cruelty, and that revenge automatically leads to more revenge. Of all the religions, Christianity is the most explicit on these matters. We are asked to forgive our enemies, turn the other cheek, and if necessary die in the process so that others will respect and follow the non-violent way. Now that we can so easily destroy the world, such teaching would seem to be the sanest way forward.